The Author's Accountability

PLANNER

A Day-by-Day Guide for Writers

"Because Writing is Hard."

2023

4 Horsemen
Publications, Inc.

Dedication

To all the great writers who continue to create amazing art with your words. We hope this helps you to achieve your dreams.

INTRODUCTION

"Guys, I need this in my life: An Author Accountability Guide."

The Researcher

"Yeah, we should do that!"

The Architect

"That's a great idea! Someone should do that!"

The Cheerleader

"And so we became Someone."

The Taskmaster

Once upon a time, there were four Muses who decided to create a planner/guide for writers. This magical book would be a new resource for those seeking to set goals, track progress (not just word count), and enjoy the Museinspired motivation to stick with it for an entire year. Thus, the Author's Accountability Planner was born and we have repeated the process every year because we need to keep ourselves on track as authors. We hope authors find this book useful through each stage of their writing journey. Writing and creating, whether full-time or part-time, require time and organization. This planner is designed to help track time, provide recommendations, and share what the Muses have discovered to be game changers on their own journeys. Throughout the year, everyone faces the challenges of self-doubt, procrastination, and Life in General. It's okay! Every week, the Muses are here to guide you through this adventure. We will get through this together.

HOW TO USE THIS BOOK

The Muses have spent countless hours fine-tuning the functionality of this book (by deciding if it should record writing time or beyond that). In the end, the Muses decided to account for all of the time spent doing writer-type things (brainstorming, writing, researching, editing, marketing, etc.). Many books discuss word count, but so much more happens before, after, and during the process of laying a book on paper (both physically and digitally).

Finishing the story is the single most important and difficult part of being a writer. To succeed, writers need accountability, someone or something to keep them motivated week after week. The Muses are here to keep the adventure moving forward, fight writer's block, and offer strategies to achieve year-end goals. Life is unpredictable, offering a variety of momentum-destroying reasons. This book can help you fight through those tough times while maintaining high morale.

In the end, only YOU can write YOUR story. You're here now, ready to do this. Let's go!

THE LAYOUT

This book contains four parts: Introductory Material (you're here!), Goal Setting, Month-by-Month Tracking, and Year Review. Each month has three sections: Monthly Prep, Weekly Overviews, and Monthly Review.

TRACKING DAILY ACCOMPLISHMENTS

Authors know that writing is more than sitting in a chair and putting words to paper (or screen). Word count is only one component of the writing process. A whole realm of prepping, marketing, research, and editing gets left out of all those other planners! We want you to be accountable by tracking all of the time you devote to your writing. Throughout this planner, the Muses have divided daily writing time into several different categories: Word Count, Brainstorming, Editing, Marketing, Research, and Reading.

Track your progress in these categories every day. It's okay to put a zero in a few places and focus on one task. Reviewing this information later can be

DAILY ACCOMPLISHMENTS	FRIDAY 29
Word Count:	Marketing Hours:
Brainstorming Hours:	Research Hours:
Editing Hours:	Reading Hours:

eye-opening when you compare good and bad weeks. In the end, use these pages to fine-tune your writing schedule, optimizing your output for all your writing needs. Some of us perform better when pairing tasks with one another; other times we reach higher word counts after reading and researching. Use these numbers to maximize your potential and make goal setting more rewarding.

WORD COUNT

You know this one! Word count is a common measure among authors to track their progress.

BRAINSTORMING

Some of us are pantsers while others are plotters. At times, we combine strategies! Either way, we spend some time prepping a story, even if it's an hour at the cafe writing on a napkin.

EDITING

Most writers work on more than one project at a time. Divide your attention between writing one work while editing another. One story might be completely drafted but still needs revision and editing. This step should never be skipped—whether posting to a blog or pitching to agents or publishers. Check your work.

MARKETING

If you dream to be famous, build awareness, or publish books, it's important to keep your author platform active by engaging on social media, writing blogs, posting advertisements, sending out newsletters, hosting events, and more. Automate as much as possible, scheduling your posts in advance to give yourself more time to create content. Don't risk losing your reader's interest!

RESEARCH

Whether researching how to buy a horse or a new method for writing dialogue, count your time. You're working! As a writer no less! These hours count too. ting. Some projects might be more demanding than others, so log your time!

READING

As writers, we hear this advice often: Read what you're writing! It's true! Read widely and often—both in and out of your comfort zone. Pick up a classic or treat yourself with the newest release. Engage in the writing world in every way.

I Want to Be a Writer

Take a look at all the projects and stories you want to complete for this coming year and predict your word count for them. It's okay to fall over or under— and you may massage these as the year progresses, but throw something out there to get started. Here's a rough scope of word counts to aid you in estimation:

TYPES	GENRE
Flash Fiction	Blog Posts
1,000 word or less	200-1,200
Short Story	Romance
1,200-10,000	50,000-70,000
Novelette	Paranormal
10,000-30,000	70,000-90,000
Novella	Fantasy
30,000-45,000	90,000-120,000
Novel	Crime
50,000-85,000	90,000-100,000
Epic Novel	Mystery/Thriller/Suspense
90,000-150,000	70,000-80,000
Textbook	Memoir
50,000-250,000	30,000-70,000
Young Adult	Science Fiction
50,000-80,000	90,000-125,000
Middle Grade	Horror
25,000-40,000	70,000-100,000
Chapter Books	Historical
10,000-20,000	80,000-120,000
Picture Books	Erotica
300-700	7,000-50,000

How many words will you write this year? _____

How many words did you complete last year? _____

How many projects will you complete? _____

Set the Official Goal:

What will you accomplish this year?

Congratulations on putting your goals into writing! You're committed to the adventure ahead. You're ready. Just a few more things while we're here.

Explain your motivation right now, in this moment, in words. Why are you doing this?

_____

_____

_____

_____

What goal(s) do you want to complete this year? Complete a novel, write a dozen short stories, or land an agent? Put it into the universe!

_____

_____

_____

_____

How are you going to accomplish this writing goal? No, really, literally write down how you will do this.

_____

_____

_____

_____

When will you be writing? (*Have set times in mind so you can establish a routine, but "whenever I can" is also a valid response! Get it done in whatever way works for you and your life.*)

_____

_____

_____

_____

Where will you be writing? (*Have you tried different places?*)

_____

_____

_____

_____

What do you need in order to write successfully? (*Fluff the pillow, cue the music, pour the drink, etc.*)

_____

_____

_____

_____

How will you be writing? (*computer, laptop, yellow legal pad, quill and ink pot, etc.*)

_____

_____

_____

_____

PLAN FOR PROBLEMS

"I am ready to face any challenges that might be foolish enough to face me!"

— Dwight Schrute (The Office)

Do some research and find writers who have experienced similar issues—what did they do to succeed? How can you use their lives/experiences as a lesson in your life?

Make a chart of obstacles that are within your control and those that are not. When you feel yourself losing momentum or focus, refer to this chart to see how you categorized the anti-writing forces in your life. If it's beyond your control, then move on; there's nothing you can do about it. Do whatever you can to get through this. But if it's something you said was controllable, think about what you can do to adjust for the issue.

What are some obstacles that prevent you from writing?

_____

How can you overcome these issues?

_____

What has prevented you from writing in the past?

_____

How will you address these known pitfalls?

_____

DO OR DO NOT

"I never look back darling! It distracts from the now."

— Edna Mode, Incredibles

There is no try? Remember that you are not a jedi. Writing is not a done/not done situation—because most writers would probably agree that writing is never done, it's just due. It could always be better with one more round of edits, one more polishing session, one more gentle nudge and subtle tweak.

Writing is a process, a journey, a path deeper into the woods. Use this book to plan how far you'd like to travel along that path this year. As Tolkien said, the road goes ever on and on, and we must follow if we can.

MOTIVATION TIME!

Are you motivated by rewards or punishment?

REWARDS: ALL OF THE PRIZES!

It doesn't matter if you win by an inch or a mile. Winning is winning.

— *Fast and the Furious*

Does the idea of a sweet prize at the end of the road get you off your phone to write? It's time to reward yourself on top of the gloating satisfaction of sweet, sweet success.

WISH LIST TIME

You deserve all the things. Tease yourself with something really cool at the end of this road.

1ST PRIZE

Make it worthwhile—something to motivate you when you don't want to write. A long-desired trip, a fancy meal, a new leather-bound hardcover that you don't need but really really really want...shoot for the stars in your life!

What will you do for yourself when you reach your goal?

_____

2ND PRIZE

This should be something cool, something you wouldn't do or get for yourself normally, but not the magical rainbow party of 1st prize. You deserve this, but you could have had that other thing—use this feeling as motivation for next time!

What will you do for yourself when you get really close to your goal?

_____

3RD PRIZE

Again, make this something nice, worthwhile, but not the awesomeness you listed above. For me, 3rd prize would be like Chili's—slightly special/different and fun, but definitely not what I could have been eating right now.

What will you do for yourself when you get remotely close to your goal?

_____

HONORABLE MENTION

This should be a consolation prize, the webcam you win in the office give-away, the free pedometer from your insurance company, something new, but definitely not what it could have been.

What will you do for yourself for taking the first few steps toward your goal?

ALL OF THE PUNISHMENTS!

"When I hear someone sigh, Life is hard, I am always tempted to ask, Compared to what?"

— *Sydney Harris*

Does the idea of an awful punishment push you out of bed to do some writing? It's time to envision the reckoning waiting for you if you fail. It's Negative Reinforcement Time: You want to accomplish your goals, but sometimes you need the threat of the blade over your neck to get it done. Threaten yourself with what will happen if you do not meet your goals. (It's really important that you set realistic goals if you plan to go this route!)

I COULD HAVE TRIED HARDER

You know it's true. It wasn't life getting in the way. It wasn't beyond your control. This is totally on you. What privilege should you lose as a result? Avoid choosing something writing-related as a punishment. Make it something you really don't want to do or deal with at all.

For example, if I blow a goal because of laziness, I have to take the stairs to my office at work. I work on the third floor, and the stairs are outside in the heat. The idea of trudging up them in the heat and humidity of a Florida summer is enough to get me out of bed and in front of my computer to write every day.

What will happen if you fail this way?

I PHONED IT IN

You know what happened. You were there, and you let it happen. You could have done it, but you did other things instead (not life-required things, but shiny objects that distracted you from your path). What privilege or perk should you lose? This could be something small to be a daily reminder of your failure or an all-in-one punishment that you'd rather not experience.

If I phone it in, I punish myself by wearing a really uncomfortable bra for a day or a week, depending on size of the goal/target. The discomfort is a constant reminder of my failure, motivating me the next time I think about phoning it in.

What should happen if you phone it in?

_____

_____

_____

I REALLY STOPPED TRYING

You know you topped even attempting to get it done. You let the magnitude of other things get in the way, and you didn't write what you wanted. (This is a good time to sit down and think about why you failed. Check out the I Failed... Now What? section). What privilege/perk should you lose for falling off the wagon? This should be more of a punishment than the previous two, something you really don't want to happen. For me, these are usually housework-cleaning related tasks. Bonus—I'm not allowed to return to my writing until my house is spotless.

What should happen if you really stop trying?

_____

_____

_____

I completely gave up

It happens. You walked away. But promises were made, and perhaps gifts were exchanged, and now you have to face the consequences. This should be serious, more than giving up your morning latte, beyond sweating over stairs or toilets. If you want the consequences method to work, this should be something you really really really don't want to experience.

Note—this isn't about berating yourself for failing, reinforcing how much you suck, or dwelling in how awful you are. Life happens. This punishment should be something you use as a proverbial sword over your neck to motivate you to write when you'd rather do anything else (even clean the toilet). My super awful worst punishment for not meeting a writing goal is living without music for an entire week. I love music—it's a huge part of my life and my makeup. I don't like a quiet house, a silent car ride, or a creepy echoing office in the evening after everyone goes home. Not having the option to cover the silence with sweet music is an awful possibility.

What should happen if you completely give up?

_____

_____

_____

Refer back to these pages periodically throughout the year. Remind yourself what you are working for—aside from the awesome, awe-inspiring feeling of finally completing a project that has haunted you for years, lingering in your brain unwritten for far too much of your life. You can totally do this!

Monthly Prep

Each month begins with planning—specific questions to make you think about the intersection between your writing and your life. Solid planning allows you to reach your goals.

For example, in November and December, writing time may be replaced with family time due to the holidays. It's okay to have smaller goals in the months with planned trips, scheduled events, or non-writing projects—when keeping normal routines is impossible. It's important for writers to be kind to themselves, finding that balance between accountability and self-flagellation.

Look at your month

How many days this month will you work on writing stuff? Consider available weekdays/weekends. Will holidays affect your writing schedule? What is scheduled in your life that might affect your writing time? It's okay to plan for time when you will NOT write. Acknowledge your situation and plan accordingly.

What project(s) will you work on?

_____

_____

_____

Announcing your plan for the month is a special feeling. You can still stray if you want, but use this space to set your expectations (so you know what to prioritize this month).

What goal are you aiming to achieve?

_____

_____

_____

Now's your chance to assign a goal. Are you planning to finish a novel? Short story? Poem? Moving into the editing stage or brainstorming a new story by the end of the month? Goals can include sending out a set number of queries, gaining new followers, or buying that workbook you wanted.

What is your biggest obstacle this month?

_____

_____

_____

Anyone can look at a month and groan. Whether it's a holiday heavy month, the family reunion, or peak season with lots of overtime at your day job—we have all been there! Take a moment to acknowledge predictable obstacles.

How will you tackle these obstacles?

_____

_____

_____

Now, decide what you will do to address these issues. Will you bring a book to read and focus on a higher reading goal this month? Maybe lower your word count goal and double down on marketing since you can do social media from your phone while at a billion doctor appointments. You've got this!

What is your End of the Month reward?

_____

_____

_____

Treat yourself! It's hard following your dreams without some encouragement along the way. Life doesn't slow down, and you've made sacrifices to achieve your goals, so give yourself a pat on the back. Go to a movie, buy a new game, or even invite a friend over for wine and cheese. Always acknowledge how far you've progressed, even if not all your goals were met.

Goals for the Month

After this reflection time, you're ready to set your goals. It's okay to adjust them according to the demands of the month. Your monthly goals should be constantly evolving based on your previous month (that's why it's next to your Monthly Review).

Weekly Overview

Every week contains tasks, questions, and tips. After many painful choices, the Muses settled on what would be most helpful for your adventure this year: something to help with writer's block, remind you of your goals, and continue rewarding your creativity (perhaps with treats). Fill in this page during the week, and finish before moving on (Yes, this book has homework). Each item was chosen to prompt critical thinking and creativity on several levels.

Exercise

Every week, set a 5-minute timer and write a short work of fiction incorporating the two words. These short activities refill the creative well. Did you write something? Head over to the 4HP Accountable Authors Group on Facebook and share your awesome words!

Questions

What was your sprint time and top word count?

Was it a 20-minute sprint with 350 words? A 5-minutes dalliance with 75 words? You're awesome! Record it here.

List favorite (or new) songs you (re)discovered this week:

Writers have a toolbox that inspires us. What is the soundtrack for your current project? The Researcher and the Architect both have many playlists specific to their series to keep them fueled. Often, they exchange songs!

Favorite food or drink this week:

What yummy food and drink did you have this week? Make sure you treat yourself on occasion. The Cheerleader enjoys trying out new teas, and the Taskmaster finds ways to reward not only herself, but fellow writers. Don't assume you have to do this alone. Eat and stay healthy. Self-care is critical. Don't neglect other parts of your life!

How did you reward yourself?

Not all of us enjoy food as a reward, so we ask...how did you reward yourself? Did you buy that item of clothing from that store? Order something cool online? Find another new book to read? Take a short trip outside? Oh, so many options here!

What project(s) did you actually work on?

Pay attention to which projects you work on. Sometimes one story will flow more easily than others. That's okay! Is there a pattern? Does a certain genre speak to you more than another? Seeing how many hours you devote to a specific project can be eye-opening.

What are you reading right now?

Write down the titles of the books you read each week. Was it a writer resource? A reference book for brainstorming? Did you reward yourself with a cozy mystery? Remember to read, exposing yourself to other writers' words.

What went well/could improve this week?

Time to get real. Evaluate your strengths and troubleshoot your weaknesses at least once a week.

Totals for the Week

Do some math. Bust out that calculator and punch it in. How did you do? Will this keep you on track to meet your monthly/yearly goals? See your progress stack up each month. Don't discredit anything! Writing is more than laying words to the page. You're not slacking when hours are spent on other facets of being an author!

Monthly Journal

Visualize where you spend your time. See how much you are doing on average and how far you've made it this year! Write down your feelings on your progress. Let it out, shout it out, and put it out there! Remind yourself how far you've made it and how far you can take it.

Monthly Review

To make it easier to find the month or circle back, we have put the month name and a color on the edge of the page. We feel it's SUPER important to look back and compare.

Questions

What was your top week this month?

There's so much that can happen in a month's time! Sit down and reflect. The Muses have pulled you into a conference room, and they're settling in to talk about how it's going (and the numbers). Don't worry—the Taskmaster is running the show, and she's already told the Researcher to focus. In fact, the Architect has pointed out some corrections while the Cheerleader is serving some tea (or coffee...or wine, depending on the month you've had).

What made your top week successful?

Looking back, it's always great to compare each week. Which one did you feel was top-notch? That's the kind of week you want to always have, one that leaves you feeling accomplished.

What made your top week successful?

What made that week so successful? Was it the reward or how you divide your time? Was there something you did differently? It's super important to be aware what made the difference so you have the ability to try to rinse and repeat.

What was your biggest obstacle?

Obstacles come in many varieties, big and small, controllable and uninvited. Acknowledge those mountains in your life and be mindful of how they influence your writing and creativity. This means you may have to change routine, maybe switch to more reading and brainstorming during these rougher climbs. It's about making your writing accountability work in your favor even in the toughest of times.

HOW DID YOU OVERCOME THIS? HOW COULD YOU IMPROVE NEXT MONTH?

Even if the answer is no, take a moment to consider strategies. Would it have been better to not worry about brainstorming and do editing or reading instead? These moments will help you tackle the next mountain.

WHAT WAS YOUR BIGGEST ACHIEVEMENT THIS MONTH?

Record the awesomeness! It can be anything and doesn't have to be something listed as a goal. Recognize what makes you feel good and boosts morale. Knowing what you can achieve makes for stronger goal setting next time.

WHAT INSPIRED YOU MOST THIS MONTH?

Inspiration comes from the most unexpected places. Track these for reference later down the road when you need a push or feel creativity slipping away. Was it a song? Something you saw in a show, movie, or documentary? Write it down! Come back to it and get recharged!

DID YOU DISCOVER A NEW WRITING TIP OR GREAT ADVICE THIS MONTH?

Writers are always learning. Advice comes in many forms, whether it's about actual writing or a fact about how to use social media in a nifty way. Write it down!

TOTAL FOR THE MONTH

Take the totals from your weeks and add those numbers up! How did you do? Did you meet a goal? Did you pass a goal? Did you not finish? These all help you plan better for the incoming month and set accurate goals.

TOTAL FOR THE YEAR

There's something satisfying about seeing how far you've come. Where are you in your journey? Do you need to adjust your weekly, monthly, or yearly goals? Don't be afraid to reassess goals. Life is unpredictable (Pandemic, anyone?). NEVER FEEL GUILTY! This is what good goal setting looks like and helps you stay on point!

COLORING GRIDS

E ach month ends with a habit wheel you can color in as well as one for the end of the year! Don't feel obligated to color something in every day, and don't be afraid to cross out and write in other options when tracking habits. We've laid a foundation based on our own experience, but this is YOUR planner! Make it work for you so you can track and collect data to make you more accountable for the activities and habits you need as a writer.

MONTHLY GRID

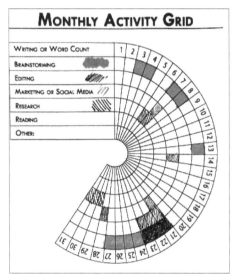

This grid is a visual graph to give you an idea which activity you favored in that month at a glance. It can also reveal if you have a tendency to "double up" tasks in the same day which can help you plan out and set new goals that match your tendencies. As you move through into a new year, looking back at these grids can help you plan for success in the years to come. Did you read a lot because of the holidays in December or was that due to other life events? Be sure to always use the journaling in conjunction to give Present You a reminder from Past You!

YEARLY GRIDS

I n the back of this amazing planner, you will find not one, but two yearly grids. These grids provide a way to visualize your achievements this year. Not only do you get to pick the colors (fancy pen time!), but you can add a handful of non-writing activities to visually compare your hobbies. At the end of the year, you can see how your time shifts to favor specific activities, especially during months with holidays or life events. Recognizing these habits allows you to set stronger goals and understand how to adjust when needed. Seeing how your time is spent (and perhaps how it could be better used) can be a game changer. Also, knowing how long certain types of projects take to complete lets you plan more effectively next time.

BY ACTIVITY

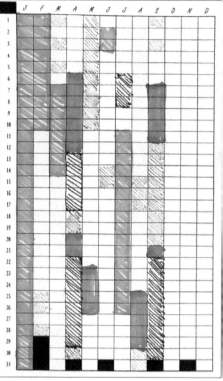

We recommend coloring in the activity you did the most that day. If there's a tie, feel free to split the box into two colors! This is taking all that data you collected on yourself and giving you a visual graph for the year. Again, it's ok to have days that are blank! Self-care, life, and setting a schedule is about recognizing when you can't work on your writing and where you can make up for it in other months. This should give you an idea of when to plan for mostly writing or mostly editing, or realize that maybe you should do a hiatus in July because you don't get much done when you try due to summer time schedule changes! We all have that section or events that cause gaps and that's ok!

BY PROJECT

A project-based grid allows you to visualize how often you worked on a project, getting a sense of how much time you spent on a project. This grid can show how long it takes for you to work on different books or writing projects. Sometimes in our grids you see where we wrote the book and after a gap filled in by other proj-

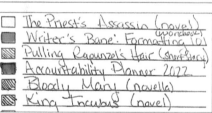

ects, we circle back to edit that project! How long do you need to edit? And how long of a break seems to benefit you the most? Was there a time you didn't work on anything? These yearly maps of our lives as writers should help you in your coming year to plan for success. That doesn't mean you won't have to adjust and plan because like is often unpredictable!

THE MUSE PAGE

We can't leave you alone. That's why every week you get a little bit of something from each muse to help you through your 7-day struggle. The content here will change up often with a combination of inspirational quotes, exercises, fun facts, writing tips, and so much more. We hope we can make you smile, take a breath, and feel inspired to keep at it. This is hard work, we know! We're writers too! We want you to find your tribe and bring awareness of the writing community to all writers looking to connect and grow!

JOIN A WRITER'S COMMUNITY

First, we'd like to invite you to join the **4HP Accountable Authors Group on Facebook**. There. You now have joined an author's community filled with folks who are actively trying to stay accountable! Also, there's a lot of writers communities out there. Check with your local library, colleges and universities, cafes, writing associations, and more.

If you prefer online, many of these have options with a variety of hashtags on Twitter and Facebook by location and genre. Find workshops, classes, or give personal experience and advice. The greatest myth is the assumption that being a writer is a solitary ordeal. No. It's not. It doesn't have to be. Now, go into the light!

NANOWRIMO.ORG

We also highly recommend joining **NaNoWriMo.org** whether you are aiming to find your local writing tribe, connect with resources, or participate in the many novel writing events in November and during Camp NaNoWriMo throughout the year. Here are some things to note that NaNo does for all authors worldwide:

- Sponsor Writing workshops year-round, especially in October!
- Hosts a Forum where you can connect and get help from fellow writers!
- Encourage kinship as we all aim to write 50,000 words in a month.
- A means to track your writing and projects!
- Access to discounts for materials and services for authors.
- Discover local libraries, clubs, and peers who run your NaNo chapter!
- Alternatives to November and the ability to set smaller goals.
- A newsletter and social media to keep you connected and in-the-know.

The Cheerleader

Hello! So great to meet you! I love supporting writers! If you can't tell, I'm excited to have you here and for the opportunity to be your muse. My goal is to send you positive vibes, inspire your creativity, and encourage you to reward yourself often. Let's make magic happen!

I write paranormal romance and fantasy. Favorite Book: The Talisman by Stephen King and Peter Straub.

THE ARCHITECT

Your prose is beautiful, and I'm here to help you keep it polished and publishable. We are building your writing together, so look for my advice and reminders at every turn. This is about mastering your craft, and you don't have to do it alone. Let's build a masterpiece together!

I write young adult epic fantasy and adult paranormal romance.
Favorite Book: The Blue Sword by Robin McKinley

THE RESEARCHER

Did you know... that I love to drop facts and encourage you to discover new things outside your comfort zone. Stimulating the brain and sparking creativity through research and the world around you is a vital part of being a writer. Whether we're investigating some hidden nugget of history or looking back at how strange life can be, let's light a fire on your imagination.

I write fantasy, paranormal, mythology, romance, and erotica.
Favorite Book: The Captive Prince Trilogy

THE TASKMASTER

Staying focused and on point can be difficult. Oftentimes writer's block can derail days if not months of effort. I'm here to keep you on task! One way to do this is through constant evaluation and setting goals. I will be here to create a sense of urgency while keeping you moving forward in one way or another. Now, let's get to work!

I write horror, paranormal, thriller, and erotica.
Favorite Book: "YOURS! As soon as you finish it!
Get to Work!"

Let the Accountability Planner Commence!

JANUARY

A new year has dawned, and the amazing muses are still here with you, ready to embark on this accountability adventure. As you take your first steps, remember the muses are here to encourage the process, enhance your skills, and eradicate your writing and editing woes. This adventure will help you set strong yet attainable writing goals this year.

Jan 1 New Year's Day　　*Jan 15 Martin Luther*　　*Jan 27 International*
Jan 8 Battle of New Orleans　　*King, Jr. Day*　　*Holocaust Remembrance Day*

What Does Your Month Look Like

Holidays:_____　　Weekends:_____
Weekdays:_____　　Other:_____

What **project(s)** do you plan on working on?

_____

What **goal** are you aiming to achieve?

_____

What will be your biggest **obstacle** this month?

_____

How will you **overcome** this? Or adjust for this?

_____

What will be your End of the Month **reward**?

_____

Goals for this Month

Word Count:_____　　Marketing Hours:_____
Brainstorming Hours:_____　　Research Hours:_____
Editing Hours:_____　　Reading Hours:_____

JANUARY

DAILY ACCOMPLISHMENTS   SUNDAY 1

WORD COUNT:_____   MARKETING HOURS:_____
BRAINSTORMING HOURS:_____ RESEARCH HOURS:_____
EDITING HOURS:_____   READING HOURS:_____

DAILY ACCOMPLISHMENTS   MONDAY 2

WORD COUNT:_____   MARKETING HOURS:_____
BRAINSTORMING HOURS:_____ RESEARCH HOURS:_____
EDITING HOURS:_____   READING HOURS:_____

DAILY ACCOMPLISHMENTS   TUESDAY 3

WORD COUNT:_____   MARKETING HOURS:_____
BRAINSTORMING HOURS:_____ RESEARCH HOURS:_____
EDITING HOURS:_____   READING HOURS:_____

DAILY ACCOMPLISHMENTS   WEDNESDAY 4

WORD COUNT:_____   MARKETING HOURS:_____
BRAINSTORMING HOURS:_____ RESEARCH HOURS:_____
EDITING HOURS:_____   READING HOURS:_____

DAILY ACCOMPLISHMENTS   THURSDAY 5

WORD COUNT:_____   MARKETING HOURS:_____
BRAINSTORMING HOURS:_____ RESEARCH HOURS:_____
EDITING HOURS:_____   READING HOURS:_____

DAILY ACCOMPLISHMENTS   FRIDAY 6

WORD COUNT:_____   MARKETING HOURS:_____
BRAINSTORMING HOURS:_____ RESEARCH HOURS:_____
EDITING HOURS:_____   READING HOURS:_____

DAILY ACCOMPLISHMENTS   SATURDAY 7

WORD COUNT:_____   MARKETING HOURS:_____
BRAINSTORMING HOURS:_____ RESEARCH HOURS:_____
EDITING HOURS:_____   READING HOURS:_____

Weekly Overview

What was your sprint time and top word count?

_____

List a new song you discovered this week:

_____

Favorite food or drink this week:

_____

How did you reward yourself?

_____

What project(s) did you work on?

_____

What are you reading?

_____

What went well this week?

_____

What could improve this week?

_____

_____

_____

Total for the Week

Word Count:_____   Marketing Hours:_____
Brainstorming Hours:_____   Research Hours:_____
Editing Hours:_____   Reading Hours:_____

Don't forget to color in your grid!

JANUARY

The Cheerleader

WHY ARE YOU HERE? What motivates your writing? Make a list of things that excite you. Use this to fuel your writing and increase your word count.

THE ARCHITECT

Explore your settings. Many software programs, including Word and Scrivener, constantly update their grammar and spelling systems. Be sure to open and adjust those options to better fit your needs during editing.

THE RESEARCHER

Get ready: we're going WAY back in time in 700 BC. Greeks and Egyptians weaved abestos into fabric. Well, mostly for tablecloths and napkins so they could clean them with fire... which caused "sickness in the lungs" for many servants. What materials are considered deadly to your world and characters? Is it something they did on accident or were they poisoned by someone else?

THE TASKMASTER

You are beginning. I am proud of you for even opening to this page. But there is so much more you are going to do this year, so let's begin.

JANUARY

5

JANUARY

DAILY ACCOMPLISHMENTS   SUNDAY 8

WORD COUNT:_____   MARKETING HOURS:_____
BRAINSTORMING HOURS:_____   RESEARCH HOURS:_____
EDITING HOURS:_____   READING HOURS:_____

DAILY ACCOMPLISHMENTS   MONDAY 9

WORD COUNT:_____   MARKETING HOURS:_____
BRAINSTORMING HOURS:_____   RESEARCH HOURS:_____
EDITING HOURS:_____   READING HOURS:_____

DAILY ACCOMPLISHMENTS   TUESDAY 10

WORD COUNT:_____   MARKETING HOURS:_____
BRAINSTORMING HOURS:_____   RESEARCH HOURS:_____
EDITING HOURS:_____   READING HOURS:_____

DAILY ACCOMPLISHMENTS   WEDNESDAY 11

WORD COUNT:_____   MARKETING HOURS:_____
BRAINSTORMING HOURS:_____   RESEARCH HOURS:_____
EDITING HOURS:_____   READING HOURS:_____

DAILY ACCOMPLISHMENTS   THURSDAY 12

WORD COUNT:_____   MARKETING HOURS:_____
BRAINSTORMING HOURS:_____   RESEARCH HOURS:_____
EDITING HOURS:_____   READING HOURS:_____

DAILY ACCOMPLISHMENTS   FRIDAY 13

WORD COUNT:_____   MARKETING HOURS:_____
BRAINSTORMING HOURS:_____   RESEARCH HOURS:_____
EDITING HOURS:_____   READING HOURS:_____

DAILY ACCOMPLISHMENTS   SATURDAY 14

WORD COUNT:_____   MARKETING HOURS:_____
BRAINSTORMING HOURS:_____   RESEARCH HOURS:_____
EDITING HOURS:_____   READING HOURS:_____

Weekly Overview

EXERCISE: Take 5-minutes to write something with the 2 words below:

Warm   Bowling

Post your exercise on the 4HP Accountable Authors Group on Facebook!

What was your sprint time and top word count?

_____

List a new song you discovered this week:

_____

Favorite food or drink this week:

_____

How did you reward yourself?

_____

What project(s) did you work on?

_____

What are you reading?

_____

What went well this week?

_____

What could improve this week?

_____

_____

_____

Total for the Week

Word Count:_____   Marketing Hours:_____

Brainstorming Hours:_____   Research Hours:_____

Editing Hours:_____   Reading Hours:_____

Don't forget to color in your grid!

The Cheerleader

What's your favorite book of all time? Why?

THE ARCHITECT

You're in the elevator with your dream publisher. In one minute, explain why your project is freaking amazing.

THE RESEARCHER

"Write the story that's in your heart and not the one you think will pay the most money."

— *Brenda Jackson*

THE TASKMASTER

Week two and you have survived so far. I hope you have your goals for this year done. If you do not, let's get them mapped. You can always adjust!

JANUARY

9

JANUARY

DAILY ACCOMPLISHMENTS   **SUNDAY 15**

WORD COUNT:_____   MARKETING HOURS:_____
BRAINSTORMING HOURS:_____ RESEARCH HOURS:_____
EDITING HOURS:_____   READING HOURS:_____

DAILY ACCOMPLISHMENTS   **MONDAY 16**

WORD COUNT:_____   MARKETING HOURS:_____
BRAINSTORMING HOURS:_____ RESEARCH HOURS:_____
EDITING HOURS:_____   READING HOURS:_____

DAILY ACCOMPLISHMENTS   **TUESDAY 17**

WORD COUNT:_____   MARKETING HOURS:_____
BRAINSTORMING HOURS:_____ RESEARCH HOURS:_____
EDITING HOURS:_____   READING HOURS:_____

DAILY ACCOMPLISHMENTS   **WEDNESDAY 18**

WORD COUNT:_____   MARKETING HOURS:_____
BRAINSTORMING HOURS:_____ RESEARCH HOURS:_____
EDITING HOURS:_____   READING HOURS:_____

DAILY ACCOMPLISHMENTS   **THURSDAY 19**

WORD COUNT:_____   MARKETING HOURS:_____
BRAINSTORMING HOURS:_____ RESEARCH HOURS:_____
EDITING HOURS:_____   READING HOURS:_____

DAILY ACCOMPLISHMENTS   **FRIDAY 20**

WORD COUNT:_____   MARKETING HOURS:_____
BRAINSTORMING HOURS:_____ RESEARCH HOURS:_____
EDITING HOURS:_____   READING HOURS:_____

DAILY ACCOMPLISHMENTS   **SATURDAY 21**

WORD COUNT:_____   MARKETING HOURS:_____
BRAINSTORMING HOURS:_____ RESEARCH HOURS:_____
EDITING HOURS:_____   READING HOURS:_____

Weekly Overview

EXERCISE: Take 5-minutes to write something with the 2 words below:

Gift   Expectations

Post your exercise on the 4HP Accountable Authors Group on Facebook!

What was your sprint time and top word count?

_____

List a new song you discovered this week:

_____

Favorite food or drink this week:

_____

How did you reward yourself?

_____

What project(s) did you work on?

_____

What are you reading?

_____

What went well this week?

_____

What could improve this week?

_____

_____

_____

Total for the Week

Word Count:_____   Marketing Hours:_____
Brainstorming Hours:_____   Research Hours:_____
Editing Hours:_____   Reading Hours:_____

Don't forget to color in your grid!

11

The Cheerleader

"If you want to be a writer, you have to write everyday. You don't go to a well just once in awhile but daily."
— *Walter Mosley*

JANUARY

THE ARCHITECT

Write under different circumstances once this week (music, background, process, etc. Shake it up somehow!). How did it go?

THE RESEARCHER

Some characters name their sword, plane, and more. In fact, naming one's ammunition was common in ancient times, but in a more dark humor way. Many slingshot balls have been found in Greece from the 4th BC era with sayings like "Take that!" or "Catch!" What would one of your characters name a weapon? Or write on an item? Add it in a story!

THE TASKMASTER

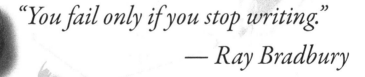

"You fail only if you stop writing."
— *Ray Bradbury*

WEEK 4

DAILY ACCOMPLISHMENTS	**SUNDAY 22**
WORD COUNT: _____	MARKETING HOURS: _____
BRAINSTORMING HOURS: _____	RESEARCH HOURS: _____
EDITING HOURS: _____	READING HOURS: _____

DAILY ACCOMPLISHMENTS	**MONDAY 23**
WORD COUNT: _____	MARKETING HOURS: _____
BRAINSTORMING HOURS: _____	RESEARCH HOURS: _____
EDITING HOURS: _____	READING HOURS: _____

DAILY ACCOMPLISHMENTS	**TUESDAY 24**
WORD COUNT: _____	MARKETING HOURS: _____
BRAINSTORMING HOURS: _____	RESEARCH HOURS: _____
EDITING HOURS: _____	READING HOURS: _____

DAILY ACCOMPLISHMENTS	**WEDNESDAY 25**
WORD COUNT: _____	MARKETING HOURS: _____
BRAINSTORMING HOURS: _____	RESEARCH HOURS: _____
EDITING HOURS: _____	READING HOURS: _____

DAILY ACCOMPLISHMENTS	**THURSDAY 26**
WORD COUNT: _____	MARKETING HOURS: _____
BRAINSTORMING HOURS: _____	RESEARCH HOURS: _____
EDITING HOURS: _____	READING HOURS: _____

DAILY ACCOMPLISHMENTS	**FRIDAY 27**
WORD COUNT: _____	MARKETING HOURS: _____
BRAINSTORMING HOURS: _____	RESEARCH HOURS: _____
EDITING HOURS: _____	READING HOURS: _____

DAILY ACCOMPLISHMENTS	**SATURDAY 28**
WORD COUNT: _____	MARKETING HOURS: _____
BRAINSTORMING HOURS: _____	RESEARCH HOURS: _____
EDITING HOURS: _____	READING HOURS: _____

Weekly Overview

What was your sprint time and top word count?

_____

List a new song you discovered this week:

_____

Favorite food or drink this week:

_____

How did you reward yourself?

_____

What project(s) did you work on?

_____

What are you reading?

_____

What went well this week?

_____

What could improve this week?

_____

_____

_____

Total for the Week

Word Count:_____   Marketing Hours:_____
Brainstorming Hours:_____   Research Hours:_____
Editing Hours:_____   Reading Hours:_____

Don't forget to color in your grid!

JANUARY

The Cheerleader

Songs are filled with helpful advice. Write down an inspiring quote here.

THE ARCHITECT

Take a moment every time you write the word "that" and read the sentence to see if you need it. If it still makes sense without it, that's one less word to edit out later!

THE RESEARCHER

"Life is pretty simple: You do some stuff. Most fails. Some works. You do more of what works. If it works big, others quickly copy it. Then you do something else. The trick is in doing something else."

— Leonardo da Vinci

THE TASKMASTER

Are you keeping up with your goals? If not, let's get back on track. Set time aside in the morning or evening just for your writing. If you need, lock your phone in the closet. It might deserve it!

JANUARY

JANUARY

DAILY ACCOMPLISHMENTS   **SUNDAY 29**

WORD COUNT:_____   MARKETING HOURS:_____
BRAINSTORMING HOURS:_____   RESEARCH HOURS:_____
EDITING HOURS:_____   READING HOURS:_____

DAILY ACCOMPLISHMENTS   **MONDAY 30**

WORD COUNT:_____   MARKETING HOURS:_____
BRAINSTORMING HOURS:_____   RESEARCH HOURS:_____
EDITING HOURS:_____   READING HOURS:_____

DAILY ACCOMPLISHMENTS   **TUESDAY 31**

WORD COUNT:_____   MARKETING HOURS:_____
BRAINSTORMING HOURS:_____   RESEARCH HOURS:_____
EDITING HOURS:_____   READING HOURS:_____

THE TASKMASTER

It is the start of the continuation of your epic adventure as an author. You may be feeling a little nervous, a bit excited, and most especially, certain you are going to rule the world by the end of 2023. You will if you remember: you can be your own worst enemy. So make sure you get out of your own way.

Weekly Overview

EXERCISE: Take 5-minutes to write something with the 2 words below:

Mute   Muse

Post your exercise on the 4HP Accountable Authors Group on Facebook!

What was your sprint time and top word count?

_____

List a new song you discovered this week:

_____

Favorite food or drink this week:

_____

How did you reward yourself?

_____

What project(s) did you work on?

_____

What are you reading?

_____

What went well this week?

_____

What could improve this week?

_____

_____

_____

Total for the Week

Word Count:_____   Marketing Hours:_____
Brainstorming Hours:_____   Research Hours:_____
Editing Hours:_____   Reading Hours:_____

Don't forget to color in your grid!

Monthly Activity Grid

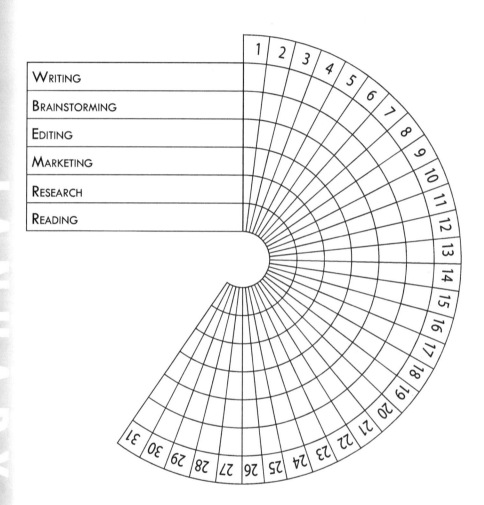

Writing

Brainstorming

Editing

Marketing

Research

Reading

Your Average Word Count for the Month

Total Word Count:_____ Divided by _____ days =_____

Total for the Year So Far

Word Count:_____
Brainstorming Hours:_____
Editing Hours:_____

Marketing Hours:_____
Research Hours:_____
Reading Hours:_____

JOURNAL

What was your **top week**?

_____

What made your **top week** successful?

_____

What was your biggest **obstacle**?

_____

How did you **overcome** this? Or could do better next time?

_____

_____

What was your biggest **achievement**?

_____

_____

What **inspired** you most this month?

_____

Did you **discover** a new writing tip or advice this month?

_____

_____

TOTAL FOR THE MONTH

Word Count:_____   Research Hours:_____
Brainstorming Hours:_____   Reading Hours:_____
Editing Hours:_____
Marketing Hours:_____

TOTAL FOR THE YEAR SO FAR

Word Count:_____   Research Hours:_____
Brainstorming Hours:_____   Reading Hours:_____
Editing Hours:_____
Marketing Hours:_____

Don't forget to color in your grid!

FEBRUARY

As you begin month two of this adventure, you should start to find your rhythm. Experts say it takes six weeks to develop a habit. Do not forget that this is your journey, and February is the month of love. Make sure you are loving yourself!

Black History Month
Feb 1 Chinese New Year
Feb 2 Groundhog Day

Feb 4 National
Wear Red Day

Feb 14 Valentine's Day
Feb 21 President's Day

WHAT DOES YOUR MONTH LOOK LIKE

Holidays:_____   Weekends:_____
Weekdays:_____   Other:_____

What **project(s)** do you plan on working on?

_____

What **goal** are you aiming to achieve?

_____

What will be your biggest **obstacle** this month?

_____

How will you **overcome** this? Or adjust for this?

_____

What will be your End of the Month **reward**?

_____

GOALS FOR THIS MONTH

Word Count:_____   Marketing Hours:_____
Brainstorming Hours:_____   Research Hours:_____
Editing Hours:_____   Reading Hours:_____

FEBRUARY

23

FEBRUARY

DAILY ACCOMPLISHMENTS   WEDNESDAY 1

WORD COUNT:_____

BRAINSTORMING HOURS:_____

EDITING HOURS:_____

MARKETING HOURS:_____

RESEARCH HOURS:_____

READING HOURS:_____

DAILY ACCOMPLISHMENTS   THURSDAY 2

WORD COUNT:_____

BRAINSTORMING HOURS:_____

EDITING HOURS:_____

MARKETING HOURS:_____

RESEARCH HOURS:_____

READING HOURS:_____

DAILY ACCOMPLISHMENTS   FRIDAY 3

WORD COUNT:_____

BRAINSTORMING HOURS:_____

EDITING HOURS:_____

MARKETING HOURS:_____

RESEARCH HOURS:_____

READING HOURS:_____

DAILY ACCOMPLISHMENTS   SATURDAY 4

WORD COUNT:_____

BRAINSTORMING HOURS:_____

EDITING HOURS:_____

MARKETING HOURS:_____

RESEARCH HOURS:_____

READING HOURS:_____

DAILY ACCOMPLISHMENTS   SUNDAY 5

WORD COUNT:_____

BRAINSTORMING HOURS:_____

EDITING HOURS:_____

MARKETING HOURS:_____

RESEARCH HOURS:_____

READING HOURS:_____

DAILY ACCOMPLISHMENTS   MONDAY 6

WORD COUNT:_____

BRAINSTORMING HOURS:_____

EDITING HOURS:_____

MARKETING HOURS:_____

RESEARCH HOURS:_____

READING HOURS:_____

DAILY ACCOMPLISHMENTS   TUESDAY 7

WORD COUNT:_____

BRAINSTORMING HOURS:_____

EDITING HOURS:_____

MARKETING HOURS:_____

RESEARCH HOURS:_____

READING HOURS:_____

Weekly Overview

EXERCISE: Take 5-minutes to write something with the 2 words below:

Calendar   Phone

Post your exercise on the 4HP Accountable Authors Group on Facebook!

What was your sprint time and top word count?

_____

List a new song you discovered this week:

_____

Favorite food or drink this week:

_____

How did you reward yourself?

_____

What project(s) did you work on?

_____

What are you reading?

_____

What went well this week?

_____

What could improve this week?

_____

_____

_____

Total for the Week

Word Count:_____   Marketing Hours:_____
Brainstorming Hours:_____   Research Hours:_____
Editing Hours:_____   Reading Hours:_____

Don't forget to color in your grid!

FEBRUARY

The Cheerleader

You're busy doubting yourself while some people are intimidated by your potential.

You're a rock star.

Let everyone see it.

THE ARCHITECT

""Find out the reason that commands you to write; see whether it has spread its roots into the very depth of your heart; confess to yourself you would have to die if you were forbidden to write."

— Rainer Maria Rilke

THE RESEARCHER

Don't touch the hair, dude! Hairstyles have always meant something through the ages. In fact, a famous ancient hairdo that was perfectly preserved was on a skull called the 'Osterby Head' and you should check it out! Does a character find their hair important? Or does hair play an important role in your worldbuilding?

THE TASKMASTER

If there is one piece of advice I can give you, it is simple... WRITE!!!!

FEBRUARY

27

DAILY ACCOMPLISHMENTS   WEDNESDAY 8

WORD COUNT:_____   MARKETING HOURS:_____
BRAINSTORMING HOURS:_____   RESEARCH HOURS:_____
EDITING HOURS:_____   READING HOURS:_____

DAILY ACCOMPLISHMENTS   THURSDAY 9

WORD COUNT:_____   MARKETING HOURS:_____
BRAINSTORMING HOURS:_____   RESEARCH HOURS:_____
EDITING HOURS:_____   READING HOURS:_____

DAILY ACCOMPLISHMENTS   FRIDAY 10

WORD COUNT:_____   MARKETING HOURS:_____
BRAINSTORMING HOURS:_____   RESEARCH HOURS:_____
EDITING HOURS:_____   READING HOURS:_____

DAILY ACCOMPLISHMENTS   SATURDAY 11

WORD COUNT:_____   MARKETING HOURS:_____
BRAINSTORMING HOURS:_____   RESEARCH HOURS:_____
EDITING HOURS:_____   READING HOURS:_____

DAILY ACCOMPLISHMENTS   SUNDAY 12

WORD COUNT:_____   MARKETING HOURS:_____
BRAINSTORMING HOURS:_____   RESEARCH HOURS:_____
EDITING HOURS:_____   READING HOURS:_____

DAILY ACCOMPLISHMENTS   MONDAY 13

WORD COUNT:_____   MARKETING HOURS:_____
BRAINSTORMING HOURS:_____   RESEARCH HOURS:_____
EDITING HOURS:_____   READING HOURS:_____

DAILY ACCOMPLISHMENTS   TUESDAY 14

WORD COUNT:_____   MARKETING HOURS:_____
BRAINSTORMING HOURS:_____   RESEARCH HOURS:_____
EDITING HOURS:_____   READING HOURS:_____

FEBRUARY

Weekly Overview

EXERCISE: Take 5-minutes to write something with the 2 words below:

Ship   Storm

Post your exercise on the 4HP Accountable Authors Group on Facebook!

What was your sprint time and top word count?

_____

List a new song you discovered this week:

_____

Favorite food or drink this week:

_____

How did you reward yourself?

_____

What project(s) did you work on?

_____

What are you reading?

_____

What went well this week?

_____

What could improve this week?

_____

_____

_____

Total for the Week

Word Count:_____   Marketing Hours:_____
Brainstorming Hours:_____   Research Hours:_____
Editing Hours:_____   Reading Hours:_____

Don't forget to color in your grid!

FEBRUARY

The Cheerleader

Who inspires you right now? Why? Who inspires your characters?

THE ARCHITECT

"The unread story is not a story; it is little black marks on wood pulp. The reader, reading it, makes it live: a live thing, a story."

— *Ursula K. Le Guin*

FEBRUARY

THE RESEARCHER

Jokes. Jesters. Jolly good times, that! That's right, the oldest joke ever discovered was a Fart Joke in Sumerian from 1900 BC about a wife not farting in her husband's lap. Through the ages, there's much fun to be had, including this zinger from the 10th century: What hangs at a man's thigh and wants to poke the hole it's often poked before? *A key!*

THE TASKMASTER

Where do you get your most creative moments? On a walk? People-watching? In the shower? Phoning a friend? Make sure when you seem stuck that you go to that happy place.

FEBRUARY

DAILY ACCOMPLISHMENTS   **WEDNESDAY 15**

WORD COUNT:_____   MARKETING HOURS:_____
BRAINSTORMING HOURS:_____   RESEARCH HOURS:_____
EDITING HOURS:_____   READING HOURS:_____

DAILY ACCOMPLISHMENTS   **THURSDAY 16**

WORD COUNT:_____   MARKETING HOURS:_____
BRAINSTORMING HOURS:_____   RESEARCH HOURS:_____
EDITING HOURS:_____   READING HOURS:_____

DAILY ACCOMPLISHMENTS   **FRIDAY 17**

WORD COUNT:_____   MARKETING HOURS:_____
BRAINSTORMING HOURS:_____   RESEARCH HOURS:_____
EDITING HOURS:_____   READING HOURS:_____

DAILY ACCOMPLISHMENTS   **SATURDAY 18**

WORD COUNT:_____   MARKETING HOURS:_____
BRAINSTORMING HOURS:_____   RESEARCH HOURS:_____
EDITING HOURS:_____   READING HOURS:_____

DAILY ACCOMPLISHMENTS   **SUNDAY 19**

WORD COUNT:_____   MARKETING HOURS:_____
BRAINSTORMING HOURS:_____   RESEARCH HOURS:_____
EDITING HOURS:_____   READING HOURS:_____

DAILY ACCOMPLISHMENTS   **MONDAY 20**

WORD COUNT:_____   MARKETING HOURS:_____
BRAINSTORMING HOURS:_____   RESEARCH HOURS:_____
EDITING HOURS:_____   READING HOURS:_____

DAILY ACCOMPLISHMENTS   **TUESDAY 21**

WORD COUNT:_____   MARKETING HOURS:_____
BRAINSTORMING HOURS:_____   RESEARCH HOURS:_____
EDITING HOURS:_____   READING HOURS:_____

FEBRUARY

WEEKLY OVERVIEW

Lamp   Uniform

What was your sprint time and top word count?

_____

List a new song you discovered this week:

_____

Favorite food or drink this week:

_____

How did you reward yourself?

_____

What project(s) did you work on?

_____

What are you reading?

_____

What went well this week?

_____

What could improve this week?

_____

_____

_____

TOTAL FOR THE WEEK

Word Count:_____   Marketing Hours:_____
Brainstorming Hours:_____   Research Hours:_____
Editing Hours:_____   Reading Hours:_____

Don't forget to color in your grid!

FEBRUARY

The Cheerleader

An author finally landed a publishing contract after 5 years of continual rejections. Who? Agatha Christie who has sold over $2 billion in books! Even the butler can see you need to keep writing!

THE ARCHITECT

Keep an eye out for "was." Rephrase the sentence to use more active verbs. Example: She was walking across the street. Alternative: She walked across the street. She strode across the street. She strut her stuff across the pavement.

THE RESEARCHER

"Be content with what you have; rejoice in the way things are. When you realize there is nothing lacking, the whole world belongs to you."

— *Lao Tzu*

THE TASKMASTER

Strike a balance between showing and telling. Unless you're writing a book about trees, or it's a vital detail to the story, nobody cares about three paragraphs describing the shape of a leaf. Find this crap and remove it. (Tolkien has strong feelings about this.)

FEBRUARY

35

Week 4

DAILY ACCOMPLISHMENTS — WEDNESDAY 22

WORD COUNT:
BRAINSTORMING HOURS:
EDITING HOURS:

MARKETING HOURS:
RESEARCH HOURS:
READING HOURS:

DAILY ACCOMPLISHMENTS — THURSDAY 23

WORD COUNT:
BRAINSTORMING HOURS:
EDITING HOURS:

MARKETING HOURS:
RESEARCH HOURS:
READING HOURS:

DAILY ACCOMPLISHMENTS — FRIDAY 24

WORD COUNT:
BRAINSTORMING HOURS:
EDITING HOURS:

MARKETING HOURS:
RESEARCH HOURS:
READING HOURS:

DAILY ACCOMPLISHMENTS — SATURDAY 25

WORD COUNT:
BRAINSTORMING HOURS:
EDITING HOURS:

MARKETING HOURS:
RESEARCH HOURS:
READING HOURS:

DAILY ACCOMPLISHMENTS — SUNDAY 26

WORD COUNT:
BRAINSTORMING HOURS:
EDITING HOURS:

MARKETING HOURS:
RESEARCH HOURS:
READING HOURS:

DAILY ACCOMPLISHMENTS — MONDAY 27

WORD COUNT:
BRAINSTORMING HOURS:
EDITING HOURS:

MARKETING HOURS:
RESEARCH HOURS:
READING HOURS:

DAILY ACCOMPLISHMENTS — TUESDAY 28

WORD COUNT:
BRAINSTORMING HOURS:
EDITING HOURS:

MARKETING HOURS:
RESEARCH HOURS:
READING HOURS:

Weekly Overview

Exercise: Take 5-minutes to write something with the 2 words below:

Medal   Key

Post your exercise on the 4HP Accountable Authors Group on Facebook!

What was your sprint time and top word count?

_____

List a new song you discovered this week:

_____

Favorite food or drink this week:

_____

How did you reward yourself?

_____

What project(s) did you work on?

_____

What are you reading?

_____

What went well this week?

_____

What could improve this week?

_____

_____

_____

Total for the Week

Word Count:_____   Marketing Hours:_____
Brainstorming Hours:_____   Research Hours:_____
Editing Hours:_____   Reading Hours:_____

Don't forget to color in your grid!

FEBRUARY

The Cheerleader

5 Minute Outline Break: Outline a project that you're thinking about. Set a timer.

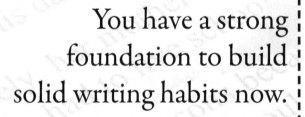

THE ARCHITECT

Two months in--look at you go!

You have a strong foundation to build solid writing habits now.

Keep it up!

FEBRUARY

38

THE RESEARCHER

War and chaos are common when looking through history, but of all of these events and changes, the collapse of the Bronze Age has been considere the worst disaster in Ancient History. Why? Several civilizations were wiped out, and they don't know why. A surge of sudden and culturally disruptive changes teamed with many natural disasters brought mankind to its knees. What kind of events could send your fictional worlds into chaos?

THE TASKMASTER

"It's the job that's never started that takes the longest to finish."

— *Samwise Gamgee (Lord of the Rings)*

You need to be writing every single day, even if it is only for 20 minutes.

FEBRUARY

MONTHLY ACTIVITY GRID

FEBRUARY

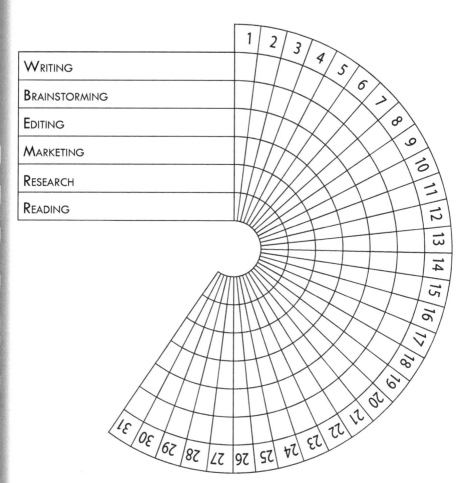

Writing
Brainstorming
Editing
Marketing
Research
Reading

YOUR AVERAGE WORD COUNT FOR THE MONTH

Total Word Count:_____ Divided by _____ days =_____

TOTAL FOR THE YEAR SO FAR

Word Count:_____   Marketing Hours:_____
Brainstorming Hours:_____   Research Hours:_____
Editing Hours:_____   Reading Hours:_____

JOURNAL

FEBRUARY

What was your **top week**?

_____

What made your **top week** successful?

_____

What was your biggest **obstacle**?

_____

How did you **overcome** this? Or could do better next time?

_____

_____

What was your biggest **achievement**?

_____

_____

What **inspired** you most this month?

_____

Did you **discover** a new writing tip or advice this month?

_____

_____

TOTAL FOR THE MONTH

Word Count:_____   Research Hours:_____
Brainstorming Hours:_____   Reading Hours:_____
Editing Hours:_____
Marketing Hours:_____

TOTAL FOR THE YEAR SO FAR

Word Count:_____   Research Hours:_____
Brainstorming Hours:_____   Reading Hours:_____
Editing Hours:_____
Marketing Hours:_____

Don't forget to color in your grid!

MARCH

N ow is the time to establish your luck for this month. If you do not see a rainbow, create it. You decide on your version of the pot of gold, but be sure to set your goals so that you can succeed. Don't forget that you can join the 4HP Accountable Authors group on Facebook and find people just like you to collaborate with. Good luck, Fellow Author!

Women's History & Irish American Heritage Month
Mar 8 International Day of Women

Mar 13 The Cheerleader's Birthday
Mar 17 St. Patrick's Day
Mar 19 The Taskmaster's Birthday

Mar 19 March Equinox
Mar 29 Good Friday
Mar 31 Easter Sunday

WHAT DOES YOUR MONTH LOOK LIKE

Holidays:_____   Weekends:_____
Weekdays:_____   Other:_____

What **project(s)** do you plan on working on?

_____

What **goal** are you aiming to achieve?

_____

What will be your biggest **obstacle** this month?

_____

How will you **overcome** this? Or adjust for this?

_____

What will be your End of the Month **reward**?

_____

GOALS FOR THIS MONTH

Word Count:_____   Marketing Hours:_____
Brainstorming Hours:_____   Research Hours:_____
Editing Hours:_____   Reading Hours:_____

WEEK 1

DAILY ACCOMPLISHMENTS	**WEDNESDAY 1**
WORD COUNT:	*MARKETING HOURS:*
BRAINSTORMING HOURS:	*RESEARCH HOURS:*
EDITING HOURS:	*READING HOURS:*

DAILY ACCOMPLISHMENTS	**THURSDAY 2**
WORD COUNT:	*MARKETING HOURS:*
BRAINSTORMING HOURS:	*RESEARCH HOURS:*
EDITING HOURS:	*READING HOURS:*

DAILY ACCOMPLISHMENTS	**FRIDAY 3**
WORD COUNT:	*MARKETING HOURS:*
BRAINSTORMING HOURS:	*RESEARCH HOURS:*
EDITING HOURS:	*READING HOURS:*

DAILY ACCOMPLISHMENTS	**SATURDAY 4**
WORD COUNT:	*MARKETING HOURS:*
BRAINSTORMING HOURS:	*RESEARCH HOURS:*
EDITING HOURS:	*READING HOURS:*

DAILY ACCOMPLISHMENTS	**SUNDAY 5**
WORD COUNT:	*MARKETING HOURS:*
BRAINSTORMING HOURS:	*RESEARCH HOURS:*
EDITING HOURS:	*READING HOURS:*

DAILY ACCOMPLISHMENTS	**MONDAY 6**
WORD COUNT:	*MARKETING HOURS:*
BRAINSTORMING HOURS:	*RESEARCH HOURS:*
EDITING HOURS:	*READING HOURS:*

DAILY ACCOMPLISHMENTS	**TUESDAY 7**
WORD COUNT:	*MARKETING HOURS:*
BRAINSTORMING HOURS:	*RESEARCH HOURS:*
EDITING HOURS:	*READING HOURS:*

WEEKLY OVERVIEW

What was your sprint time and top word count?

_____

List a new song you discovered this week:

_____

Favorite food or drink this week:

_____

How did you reward yourself?

_____

What project(s) did you work on?

_____

What are you reading?

_____

What went well this week?

_____

What could improve this week?

_____

_____

_____

TOTAL FOR THE WEEK

Word Count:_____   Marketing Hours:_____
Brainstorming Hours:_____   Research Hours:_____
Editing Hours:_____   Reading Hours:_____

Don't forget to color in your grid!

M A R C H

The Cheerleader

"Art Time: Sketch yourself reaching your year end writing goals. Visualization helps with motivation!

THE ARCHITECT

Keep it Active: Add a phrase after your sentence such as "by bunnies." (The car was driven into the field by bunnies.) If it makes sense, the sentence is passive. Consider revising to be more active. (The bunnies drove the car into the field.) When bunnies (or kitties or zombies) don't make sense, you've got it!

THE RESEARCHER

"A writer is someone for whom writing is more difficult than it is for other people."

— *Thomas Mann*

THE TASKMASTER

When was the last time you read a book in the genre you are writing? You should be doing this constantly. It helps you know what you like and do not like about the style of storytelling. Knowledge is power!

MARCH

47

WEEK 2

DAILY ACCOMPLISHMENTS   WEDNESDAY 8

WORD COUNT:_____   MARKETING HOURS:_____
BRAINSTORMING HOURS:_____   RESEARCH HOURS:_____
EDITING HOURS:_____   READING HOURS:_____

DAILY ACCOMPLISHMENTS   THURSDAY 9

WORD COUNT:_____   MARKETING HOURS:_____
BRAINSTORMING HOURS:_____   RESEARCH HOURS:_____
EDITING HOURS:_____   READING HOURS:_____

DAILY ACCOMPLISHMENTS   FRIDAY 10

WORD COUNT:_____   MARKETING HOURS:_____
BRAINSTORMING HOURS:_____   RESEARCH HOURS:_____
EDITING HOURS:_____   READING HOURS:_____

DAILY ACCOMPLISHMENTS   SATURDAY 11

WORD COUNT:_____   MARKETING HOURS:_____
BRAINSTORMING HOURS:_____   RESEARCH HOURS:_____
EDITING HOURS:_____   READING HOURS:_____

DAILY ACCOMPLISHMENTS   SUNDAY 12

WORD COUNT:_____   MARKETING HOURS:_____
BRAINSTORMING HOURS:_____   RESEARCH HOURS:_____
EDITING HOURS:_____   READING HOURS:_____

DAILY ACCOMPLISHMENTS   MONDAY 13

WORD COUNT:_____   MARKETING HOURS:_____
BRAINSTORMING HOURS:_____   RESEARCH HOURS:_____
EDITING HOURS:_____   READING HOURS:_____

DAILY ACCOMPLISHMENTS   TUESDAY 14

WORD COUNT:_____   MARKETING HOURS:_____
BRAINSTORMING HOURS:_____   RESEARCH HOURS:_____
EDITING HOURS:_____   READING HOURS:_____

Weekly Overview

What was your sprint time and top word count?

_____

List a new song you discovered this week:

_____

Favorite food or drink this week:

_____

How did you reward yourself?

_____

What project(s) did you work on?

_____

What are you reading?

_____

What went well this week?

_____

What could improve this week?

_____

_____

_____

Total for the Week

Word Count:_____   Marketing Hours:_____
Brainstorming Hours:_____   Research Hours:_____
Editing Hours:_____   Reading Hours:_____

Don't forget to color in your grid!

MARCH

M A R C H

The Cheerleader

Art time: Draw a map for your project. It can be a town, a city, a galaxy, a river system, an underground web of tunnels, or a map to buried treasure-- whatever works for you!

THE ARCHITECT

Doing sprints for 10, 20, or 30 minutes at a time will keep your writing at a good pace. Take a moment and try each out! Record your word count and figure out which is the sweet spot. Did you do better sprinting three rounds of 10 minutes with a 5 minute break between or two rounds of 30 minutes with a 10 minute break? Try a few ways and establish a routine.

THE RESEARCHER

Speaking of Bronze Age, did you ever wonder why iron weapons took over? It wasn't because they were harder and stronger. No, what made that swing in history was the simplest of facts: iron was everywhere. That's right. They made the swap because finding iron was far easier than other metals! Put a twist in your story that changes the reasoning of how they came to the stronger conclusion or just a moment of pure luck.

THE TASKMASTER

Have you written a review for the last book you read? If not, do that now. If you want reviews for your writing, and you do, then make sure you give in kind. However, if you find an issue, reach out to the author directly. It is a professional courtesy.

MARCH

MARCH

DAILY ACCOMPLISHMENTS   **WEDNESDAY 15**

WORD COUNT:_____   MARKETING HOURS:_____
BRAINSTORMING HOURS:_____   RESEARCH HOURS:_____
EDITING HOURS:_____ READING HOURS:_____

DAILY ACCOMPLISHMENTS   **THURSDAY 16**

WORD COUNT:_____   MARKETING HOURS:_____
BRAINSTORMING HOURS:_____   RESEARCH HOURS:_____
EDITING HOURS:_____ READING HOURS:_____

DAILY ACCOMPLISHMENTS   **FRIDAY 17**

WORD COUNT:_____   MARKETING HOURS:_____
BRAINSTORMING HOURS:_____   RESEARCH HOURS:_____
EDITING HOURS:_____ READING HOURS:_____

DAILY ACCOMPLISHMENTS   **SATURDAY 18**

WORD COUNT:_____   MARKETING HOURS:_____
BRAINSTORMING HOURS:_____   RESEARCH HOURS:_____
EDITING HOURS:_____ READING HOURS:_____

DAILY ACCOMPLISHMENTS   **SUNDAY 19**

WORD COUNT:_____   MARKETING HOURS:_____
BRAINSTORMING HOURS:_____   RESEARCH HOURS:_____
EDITING HOURS:_____ READING HOURS:_____

DAILY ACCOMPLISHMENTS   **MONDAY 20**

WORD COUNT:_____   MARKETING HOURS:_____
BRAINSTORMING HOURS:_____   RESEARCH HOURS:_____
EDITING HOURS:_____ READING HOURS:_____

DAILY ACCOMPLISHMENTS   **TUESDAY 21**

WORD COUNT:_____   MARKETING HOURS:_____
BRAINSTORMING HOURS:_____   RESEARCH HOURS:_____
EDITING HOURS:_____ READING HOURS:_____

Weekly Overview

EXERCISE: Take 5-minutes to write something with the 2 words below:

Horse   Smiling

Post your exercise on the 4HP Accountable Authors Group on Facebook!

What was your sprint time and top word count?

_____

List a new song you discovered this week:

_____

Favorite food or drink this week:

_____

How did you reward yourself?

_____

What project(s) did you work on?

_____

What are you reading?

_____

What went well this week?

_____

What could improve this week?

_____

_____

_____

Total for the Week

Word Count:_____   Marketing Hours:_____
Brainstorming Hours:_____   Research Hours:_____
Editing Hours:_____   Reading Hours:_____

Don't forget to color in your grid!

MARCH

MARCH

The Cheerleader

Take a moment to do some self-care and change up your surroundings. Every so often it's good to clean up your workstation, splurge to buy a new keyboard or pen, and rearrange your area for a fresh vibe to bring it back to life!

THE ARCHITECT

Follow two other writers on social media who are writing in the same genre! If they can make it happen, so can you!

THE RESEARCHER

"What we are today comes from our thoughts of yesterday, and our present thoughts build our life of tomorrow. Our life is the creation of our mind."

— *Gautama Buddha*

THE TASKMASTER

Pitch your book in 15 seconds or less. Say it out loud. Can you do it? If not, practice in front of a mirror or to another person. It's important to memorize the elevator pitch. Someone will eventually say, "What is your book about?"

MARCH

WEEK 4

DAILY ACCOMPLISHMENTS	WEDNESDAY 22
WORD COUNT:	MARKETING HOURS:
BRAINSTORMING HOURS:	RESEARCH HOURS:
EDITING HOURS:	READING HOURS:

DAILY ACCOMPLISHMENTS	THURSDAY 23
WORD COUNT:	MARKETING HOURS:
BRAINSTORMING HOURS:	RESEARCH HOURS:
EDITING HOURS:	READING HOURS:

DAILY ACCOMPLISHMENTS	FRIDAY 24
WORD COUNT:	MARKETING HOURS:
BRAINSTORMING HOURS:	RESEARCH HOURS:
EDITING HOURS:	READING HOURS:

DAILY ACCOMPLISHMENTS	SATURDAY 25
WORD COUNT:	MARKETING HOURS:
BRAINSTORMING HOURS:	RESEARCH HOURS:
EDITING HOURS:	READING HOURS:

DAILY ACCOMPLISHMENTS	SUNDAY 26
WORD COUNT:	MARKETING HOURS:
BRAINSTORMING HOURS:	RESEARCH HOURS:
EDITING HOURS:	READING HOURS:

DAILY ACCOMPLISHMENTS	MONDAY 27
WORD COUNT:	MARKETING HOURS:
BRAINSTORMING HOURS:	RESEARCH HOURS:
EDITING HOURS:	READING HOURS:

DAILY ACCOMPLISHMENTS	TUESDAY 28
WORD COUNT:	MARKETING HOURS:
BRAINSTORMING HOURS:	RESEARCH HOURS:
EDITING HOURS:	READING HOURS:

WEEKLY OVERVIEW

EXERCISE: Take 5-minutes to write something with the 2 words below:

Candle   Book

Post your exercise on the 4HP Accountable Authors Group on Facebook!

What was your sprint time and top word count?

_____

List a new song you discovered this week:

_____

Favorite food or drink this week:

_____

How did you reward yourself?

_____

What project(s) did you work on?

_____

What are you reading?

_____

What went well this week?

_____

What could improve this week?

_____

_____

_____

TOTAL FOR THE WEEK

Word Count:_____   Marketing Hours:_____
Brainstorming Hours:_____   Research Hours:_____
Editing Hours:_____   Reading Hours:_____

Don't forget to color in your grid!

MARCH

The Cheerleader

"*I have been successful probably because I have always realized that I knew nothing about writing and have merely tried to tell an interesting story entertainingly.*"
— *Edgar Rice Burroughs*

THE ARCHITECT

Weave subtext throughout your writing. This will give your story a layered, nuanced message that isn't shoved into the reader's face.

M A R C H

THE RESEARCHER

Human nature doesn't always change. For example, graffiti has always been a staple in society including in Ancient Rome where the walls were covered with the same tags we often see and in the same spots! A great place to see this is in Pompeii where travelling friends wrote in rememberance next to a bar, a classic "Sanius to Cornelius: Go hang yourself!" or the all-too-familiar "Caesius faithfully loves M..." What graffiti does your character see on the walls in their world? Or are they the type to tag walls?

THE TASKMASTER

You can be your worst critic (enemy). STOP IT!!!

You're awesome. I believe in you and in case you are wondering, your writing is amazing!

MARCH

59

DAILY ACCOMPLISHMENTS WEDNESDAY 29

WORD COUNT:_____ MARKETING HOURS:_____
BRAINSTORMING HOURS:_____ RESEARCH HOURS:_____
EDITING HOURS:_____ READING HOURS:_____

DAILY ACCOMPLISHMENTS THURSDAY 30

WORD COUNT:_____ MARKETING HOURS:_____
BRAINSTORMING HOURS:_____ RESEARCH HOURS:_____
EDITING HOURS:_____ READING HOURS:_____

DAILY ACCOMPLISHMENTS FRIDAY 31

WORD COUNT:_____ MARKETING HOURS:_____
BRAINSTORMING HOURS:_____ RESEARCH HOURS:_____
EDITING HOURS:_____ READING HOURS:_____

The Cheerleader

Have you found writers groups online or in your area? If not, start looking. Finding your tribe can be the most helpful part of this journey. Look for writers workshops, open mics, and writing and publishing conferences in your home town (or virtually). Although writing can be solitary, you don't have to do it alone! You will be amazed at all of the writing comrades you will find!

WEEKLY OVERVIEW

Studious   Fence

What was your sprint time and top word count?

_____

List a new song you discovered this week:

_____

Favorite food or drink this week:

_____

How did you reward yourself?

_____

What project(s) did you work on?

_____

What are you reading?

_____

What went well this week?

_____

What could improve this week?

_____

_____

_____

TOTAL FOR THE WEEK

Word Count:_____   Marketing Hours:_____

Brainstorming Hours:_____   Research Hours:_____

Editing Hours:_____   Reading Hours:_____

Don't forget to color in your grid!

MARCH

MONTHLY ACTIVITY GRID

MARCH

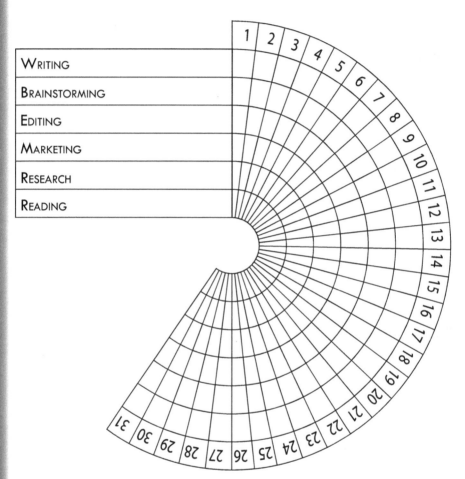

WRITING

BRAINSTORMING

EDITING

MARKETING

RESEARCH

READING

YOUR AVERAGE WORD COUNT FOR THE MONTH

Total Word Count:_____ Divided by _____ days =_____

TOTAL FOR THE YEAR SO FAR

Word Count:_____   Marketing Hours:_____

Brainstorming Hours:_____   Research Hours:_____

Editing Hours:_____   Reading Hours:_____

JOURNAL

MARCH

What was your **top week**?

_____

What made your **top week** successful?

_____

What was your biggest **obstacle**?

_____

How did you **overcome** this? Or could do better next time?

_____

_____

What was your biggest **achievement**?

_____

_____

What **inspired** you most this month?

_____

Did you **discover** a new writing tip or advice this month?

_____

_____

TOTAL FOR THE MONTH

Word Count:_____   Research Hours:_____
Brainstorming Hours:_____   Reading Hours:_____
Editing Hours:_____
Marketing Hours:_____

TOTAL FOR THE YEAR SO FAR

Word Count:_____   Research Hours:_____
Brainstorming Hours:_____   Reading Hours:_____
Editing Hours:_____
Marketing Hours:_____

Don't forget to color in your grid!

APRIL

April is a month of new beginnings. Spring is in full swing, and new animals emerge into the world. Make sure you take some time to step outside and see the world blooming around you. Who knows who or what might be right outside your door?

Apr 1 April Fool's Day
Apr 9 National Library Workers Day

Apr 15 Boston Marathon
Apr 24 Administrative Professionals Day

Apr 27 Take our Daughters and Sons to Work Day

WHAT DOES YOUR MONTH LOOK LIKE

Holidays:_____   Weekends:_____

Weekdays:_____   Other:_____

What **project(s)** do you plan on working on?

_____

What **goal** are you aiming to achieve?

_____

What will be your biggest **obstacle** this month?

_____

How will you **overcome** this? Or adjust for this?

_____

What will be your End of the Month **reward**?

_____

GOALS FOR THIS MONTH

Word Count:_____   Marketing Hours:_____

Brainstorming Hours:_____   Research Hours:_____

Editing Hours:_____   Reading Hours:_____

WEEK 1

DAILY ACCOMPLISHMENTS	SATURDAY 1
Word Count:	*Marketing Hours:*
Brainstorming Hours:	*Research Hours:*
Editing Hours:	*Reading Hours:*

DAILY ACCOMPLISHMENTS	SUNDAY 2
Word Count:	*Marketing Hours:*
Brainstorming Hours:	*Research Hours:*
Editing Hours:	*Reading Hours:*

DAILY ACCOMPLISHMENTS	MONDAY 3
Word Count:	*Marketing Hours:*
Brainstorming Hours:	*Research Hours:*
Editing Hours:	*Reading Hours:*

DAILY ACCOMPLISHMENTS	TUESDAY 4
Word Count:	*Marketing Hours:*
Brainstorming Hours:	*Research Hours:*
Editing Hours:	*Reading Hours:*

DAILY ACCOMPLISHMENTS	WEDNESDAY 5
Word Count:	*Marketing Hours:*
Brainstorming Hours:	*Research Hours:*
Editing Hours:	*Reading Hours:*

DAILY ACCOMPLISHMENTS	THURSDAY 6
Word Count:	*Marketing Hours:*
Brainstorming Hours:	*Research Hours:*
Editing Hours:	*Reading Hours:*

DAILY ACCOMPLISHMENTS	FRIDAY 7
Word Count:	*Marketing Hours:*
Brainstorming Hours:	*Research Hours:*
Editing Hours:	*Reading Hours:*

APRIL

WEEKLY OVERVIEW

EXERCISE: Take 5-minutes to write something with the 2 words below:

Bread   Swimming

Post your exercise on the 4HP Accountable Authors Group on Facebook!

What was your sprint time and top word count?

_____

List a new song you discovered this week:

_____

Favorite food or drink this week:

_____

How did you reward yourself?

_____

What project(s) did you work on?

_____

What are you reading?

_____

What went well this week?

_____

What could improve this week?

_____

_____

_____

TOTAL FOR THE WEEK

Word Count:_____   Marketing Hours:_____
Brainstorming Hours:_____   Research Hours:_____
Editing Hours:_____   Reading Hours:_____

Don't forget to color in your grid!

APRIL

The Cheerleader

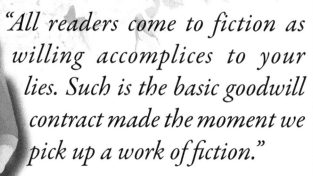

"All readers come to fiction as willing accomplices to your lies. Such is the basic goodwill contract made the moment we pick up a work of fiction."

— Steve Almond, WD

THE ARCHITECT

Five Minute Break Time: Stand up. Walk around. Go outside if you can. Look skyward, study a different wall, check out a new space. Set a timer, then return to writing when it goes off.

THE RESEARCHER

How does writing work in your world? It's not often that we stop to think of the impact of showing something we use for communication every day, but it can be a great way to show the development of the world or even the limitations of the character. Are they just painting pictures on cave walls? Or have they developed technical advances and can link via a chip in their heads?

THE TASKMASTER

"You don't have to be great to start, but you have to start to be great."

— *Zig Ziglar*

Are you maintaining your monthly goals? You're in control of that. Treat this with the same passion you want your readers to feel about your work.

APRIL

WEEK 2

DAILY ACCOMPLISHMENTS	**SATURDAY 8**
WORD COUNT: _____	MARKETING HOURS: _____
BRAINSTORMING HOURS: _____	RESEARCH HOURS: _____
EDITING HOURS: _____	READING HOURS: _____

DAILY ACCOMPLISHMENTS	**SUNDAY 9**
WORD COUNT: _____	MARKETING HOURS: _____
BRAINSTORMING HOURS: _____	RESEARCH HOURS: _____
EDITING HOURS: _____	READING HOURS: _____

DAILY ACCOMPLISHMENTS	**MONDAY 10**
WORD COUNT: _____	MARKETING HOURS: _____
BRAINSTORMING HOURS: _____	RESEARCH HOURS: _____
EDITING HOURS: _____	READING HOURS: _____

DAILY ACCOMPLISHMENTS	**TUESDAY 11**
WORD COUNT: _____	MARKETING HOURS: _____
BRAINSTORMING HOURS: _____	RESEARCH HOURS: _____
EDITING HOURS: _____	READING HOURS: _____

DAILY ACCOMPLISHMENTS	**WEDNESDAY 12**
WORD COUNT: _____	MARKETING HOURS: _____
BRAINSTORMING HOURS: _____	RESEARCH HOURS: _____
EDITING HOURS: _____	READING HOURS: _____

DAILY ACCOMPLISHMENTS	**THURSDAY 13**
WORD COUNT: _____	MARKETING HOURS: _____
BRAINSTORMING HOURS: _____	RESEARCH HOURS: _____
EDITING HOURS: _____	READING HOURS: _____

DAILY ACCOMPLISHMENTS	**FRIDAY 14**
WORD COUNT: _____	MARKETING HOURS: _____
BRAINSTORMING HOURS: _____	RESEARCH HOURS: _____
EDITING HOURS: _____	READING HOURS: _____

EXERCISE: Take 5-minutes to write something with the 2 words below:

Rope   Shorts

Post your exercise on the 4HP Accountable Authors Group on Facebook!

What was your sprint time and top word count?

_____

List a new song you discovered this week:

_____

Favorite food or drink this week:

_____

How did you reward yourself?

_____

What project(s) did you work on?

_____

What are you reading?

_____

What went well this week?

_____

What could improve this week?

_____

_____

_____

TOTAL FOR THE WEEK

Word Count:_____   Marketing Hours:_____
Brainstorming Hours:_____   Research Hours:_____
Editing Hours:_____   Reading Hours:_____

Don't forget to color in your grid!

The Cheerleader

Find something that "Sparks Joy" and keep it within sight of your writing space. Sometimes you need a gentle reminder to stay positive.

THE ARCHITECT

Sensory Overload: Describe your surroundings by using all five senses.

APRIL

THE RESEARCHER

"When you are inspired by some great purpose, some extraordinary project, all your thoughts break their bonds."

— Patanjali

THE TASKMASTER

Pick up or discover a new book on writing. You would be amazed at how many of your favorite authors have written books on writing. Continuing to learn is part of getting better at anything you do.

APRIL

APRIL

DAILY ACCOMPLISHMENTS — SATURDAY 15

WORD COUNT:_____
BRAINSTORMING HOURS:_____
EDITING HOURS:_____

MARKETING HOURS:_____
RESEARCH HOURS:_____
READING HOURS:_____

DAILY ACCOMPLISHMENTS — SUNDAY 16

WORD COUNT:_____
BRAINSTORMING HOURS:_____
EDITING HOURS:_____

MARKETING HOURS:_____
RESEARCH HOURS:_____
READING HOURS:_____

DAILY ACCOMPLISHMENTS — MONDAY 17

WORD COUNT:_____
BRAINSTORMING HOURS:_____
EDITING HOURS:_____

MARKETING HOURS:_____
RESEARCH HOURS:_____
READING HOURS:_____

DAILY ACCOMPLISHMENTS — TUESDAY 18

WORD COUNT:_____
BRAINSTORMING HOURS:_____
EDITING HOURS:_____

MARKETING HOURS:_____
RESEARCH HOURS:_____
READING HOURS:_____

DAILY ACCOMPLISHMENTS — WEDNESDAY 19

WORD COUNT:_____
BRAINSTORMING HOURS:_____
EDITING HOURS:_____

MARKETING HOURS:_____
RESEARCH HOURS:_____
READING HOURS:_____

DAILY ACCOMPLISHMENTS — THURSDAY 20

WORD COUNT:_____
BRAINSTORMING HOURS:_____
EDITING HOURS:_____

MARKETING HOURS:_____
RESEARCH HOURS:_____
READING HOURS:_____

DAILY ACCOMPLISHMENTS — FRIDAY 21

WORD COUNT:_____
BRAINSTORMING HOURS:_____
EDITING HOURS:_____

MARKETING HOURS:_____
RESEARCH HOURS:_____
READING HOURS:_____

WEEKLY OVERVIEW

EXERCISE: Take 5-minutes to write something with the 2 words below:

Hammock   Bookcase

Post your exercise on the 4HP Accountable Authors Group on Facebook!

What was your sprint time and top word count?

_____

List a new song you discovered this week:

_____

Favorite food or drink this week:

_____

How did you reward yourself?

_____

What project(s) did you work on?

_____

What are you reading?

_____

What went well this week?

_____

What could improve this week?

_____

_____

_____

TOTAL FOR THE WEEK

Word Count:_____   Marketing Hours:_____
Brainstorming Hours:_____   Research Hours:_____
Editing Hours:_____   Reading Hours:_____

Don't forget to color in your grid!

APRIL

APRIL

The Cheerleader
"You don't actually have to write anything until you've thought it out. This is an enormous relief, and you can sit there searching for the point at which the story becomes a toboggan and starts to slide."
— Marie de Nervaud

THE ARCHITECT

Time to Ctrl F your overused words. List the troublesome words here that keep sneaking back in.

THE RESEARCHER

Medicine. It's a vital aspect in life and culture. Even the ancient Egyptians wrote down their recipes and even sent copies to the library in Alexandria. Depending on your character's development, you might want to decide how much medical knowledge they have or lack.

THE TASKMASTER

How do you track your ideas? A journal is a great way to ensure you never lose a story idea. You can also use notes in your phone or voice memos. Never lose the awesomeness your imagination is generating.

APRIL

APRIL

DAILY ACCOMPLISHMENTS   **SATURDAY 22**

WORD COUNT:_____

BRAINSTORMING HOURS:_____

EDITING HOURS:_____

MARKETING HOURS:_____

RESEARCH HOURS:_____

READING HOURS:_____

DAILY ACCOMPLISHMENTS   **SUNDAY 23**

WORD COUNT:_____

BRAINSTORMING HOURS:_____

EDITING HOURS:_____

MARKETING HOURS:_____

RESEARCH HOURS:_____

READING HOURS:_____

DAILY ACCOMPLISHMENTS   **MONDAY 24**

WORD COUNT:_____

BRAINSTORMING HOURS:_____

EDITING HOURS:_____

MARKETING HOURS:_____

RESEARCH HOURS:_____

READING HOURS:_____

DAILY ACCOMPLISHMENTS   **TUESDAY 25**

WORD COUNT:_____

BRAINSTORMING HOURS:_____

EDITING HOURS:_____

MARKETING HOURS:_____

RESEARCH HOURS:_____

READING HOURS:_____

DAILY ACCOMPLISHMENTS   **WEDNESDAY 26**

WORD COUNT:_____

BRAINSTORMING HOURS:_____

EDITING HOURS:_____

MARKETING HOURS:_____

RESEARCH HOURS:_____

READING HOURS:_____

DAILY ACCOMPLISHMENTS   **THURSDAY 27**

WORD COUNT:_____

BRAINSTORMING HOURS:_____

EDITING HOURS:_____

MARKETING HOURS:_____

RESEARCH HOURS:_____

READING HOURS:_____

DAILY ACCOMPLISHMENTS   **FRIDAY 28**

WORD COUNT:_____

BRAINSTORMING HOURS:_____

EDITING HOURS:_____

MARKETING HOURS:_____

RESEARCH HOURS:_____

READING HOURS:_____

EXERCISE: Take 5-minutes to write something with the 2 words below:

Chocolate   Couch

Post your exercise on the 4HP Accountable Authors Group on Facebook!

What was your sprint time and top word count?

_____

List a new song you discovered this week:

_____

Favorite food or drink this week:

_____

How did you reward yourself?

_____

What project(s) did you work on?

_____

What are you reading?

_____

What went well this week?

_____

What could improve this week?

_____

_____

_____

TOTAL FOR THE WEEK

Word Count:_____   Marketing Hours:_____
Brainstorming Hours:_____   Research Hours:_____
Editing Hours:_____   Reading Hours:_____

Don't forget to color in your grid!

APRIL

The Cheerleader

What is your favorite way to write? Sometimes listening to music from the time or place you're writing about will get you into your character's headspace quicker. Give it a try!

THE ARCHITECT

"If something isn't working, if you have a story that you've built and it's blocked and you can't figure it out, take your favorite scene, or your very best idea or set-piece, and cut it. It's brutal, but sometimes inevitable."

— *Joss Whedon*

THE RESEARCHER

Buildings are vital in life: shelters, places of business, and study are among them. When they are destroyed or renovated, folks have found symbols, messages, items, money, and even the occasional body. Not everything has to be easily seen or found in your world.

THE TASKMASTER

I know that writing is hard. However, you are a tough person. I know you can show those words who is boss!

APRIL

DAILY ACCOMPLISHMENTS   **SATURDAY 29**

*WORD COUNT:*_____   *MARKETING HOURS:*_____
*BRAINSTORMING HOURS:*_____   *RESEARCH HOURS:*_____
*EDITING HOURS:*_____   *READING HOURS:*_____

DAILY ACCOMPLISHMENTS   **SUNDAY 30**

*WORD COUNT:*_____   *MARKETING HOURS:*_____
*BRAINSTORMING HOURS:*_____   *RESEARCH HOURS:*_____
*EDITING HOURS:*_____   *READING HOURS:*_____

APRIL

THE ARCHITECT

"Find podcasts about authors, writing, even book reviews in genres similar to your own. Get to know your fellow authors! (*We recommend starting with Drinking with Authors*).

Listen to it as you go outside for a walk or while doing chores.

Exercise is important. Self-care has to be part of your day-to-day routine. So while you are at it, learn more about the writing and publishing process.

Learning more about writing is important too!"

Weekly Overview

EXERCISE: Take 5-minutes to write something with the 2 words below:

Camera   Marshmallow

Post your exercise on the 4HP Accountable Authors Group on Facebook!

What was your sprint time and top word count?

_____

List a new song you discovered this week:

_____

Favorite food or drink this week:

_____

How did you reward yourself?

_____

What project(s) did you work on?

_____

What are you reading?

_____

What went well this week?

_____

What could improve this week?

_____

_____

_____

Total for the Week

Word Count:_____   Marketing Hours:_____

Brainstorming Hours:_____   Research Hours:_____

Editing Hours:_____   Reading Hours:_____

Don't forget to color in your grid!

MONTHLY ACTIVITY GRID

APRIL

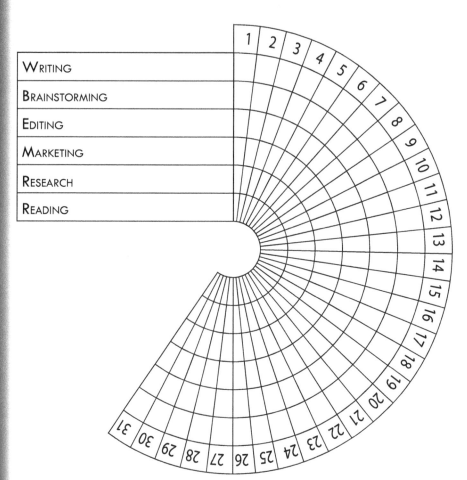

WRITING

BRAINSTORMING

EDITING

MARKETING

RESEARCH

READING

YOUR AVERAGE WORD COUNT FOR THE MONTH

Total Word Count:_____ Divided by _____ days =_____

TOTAL FOR THE YEAR SO FAR

Word Count:_____   Marketing Hours:_____
Brainstorming Hours:_____   Research Hours:_____
Editing Hours:_____   Reading Hours:_____

JOURNAL

What was your **top week**?

_____

What made your **top week** successful?

_____

What was your biggest **obstacle**?

_____

How did you **overcome** this? Or could do better next time?

_____

_____

What was your biggest **achievement**?

_____

_____

What **inspired** you most this month?

_____

Did you **discover** a new writing tip or advice this month?

_____

_____

TOTAL FOR THE MONTH

Word Count:_____   Research Hours:_____
Brainstorming Hours:_____   Reading Hours:_____
Editing Hours:_____
Marketing Hours:_____

TOTAL FOR THE YEAR SO FAR

Word Count:_____   Research Hours:_____
Brainstorming Hours:_____   Reading Hours:_____
Editing Hours:_____
Marketing Hours:_____

Don't forget to color in your grid!

MAY

The school year may almost be over. You might have to attend a graduation or be graduating yourself. Do not let that slow you down. Maybe grab your laptop, go write outside, and enjoy all that nature around you inspires. Or if you live somewhere warm, maybe it's time to disappear into some air conditioning with an iced drink!

Asian Pacific American Heritage & Jewish American Heritage Month

May 5 Cinco de Mayo
May 7 National Teacher Appreciation Day
May 12 Mother's Day

May 22 National Maritime Day
May 27 Memorial Day

WHAT DOES YOUR MONTH LOOK LIKE

Holidays:_____   Weekends:_____
Weekdays:_____   Other:_____

What **project(s)** do you plan on working on?

_____

What **goal** are you aiming to achieve?

_____

What will be your biggest **obstacle** this month?

_____

How will you **overcome** this? Or adjust for this?

_____

What will be your End of the Month **reward**?

_____

GOALS FOR THIS MONTH

Word Count:_____   Marketing Hours:_____
Brainstorming Hours:_____   Research Hours:_____
Editing Hours:_____   Reading Hours:_____

Week 1

DAILY ACCOMPLISHMENTS   **MONDAY 1**

Word Count: _____
Brainstorming Hours: _____
Editing Hours: _____

Marketing Hours: _____
Research Hours: _____
Reading Hours: _____

DAILY ACCOMPLISHMENTS   **TUESDAY 2**

Word Count: _____
Brainstorming Hours: _____
Editing Hours: _____

Marketing Hours: _____
Research Hours: _____
Reading Hours: _____

DAILY ACCOMPLISHMENTS   **WEDNESDAY 3**

Word Count: _____
Brainstorming Hours: _____
Editing Hours: _____

Marketing Hours: _____
Research Hours: _____
Reading Hours: _____

DAILY ACCOMPLISHMENTS   **THURSDAY 4**

Word Count: _____
Brainstorming Hours: _____
Editing Hours: _____

Marketing Hours: _____
Research Hours: _____
Reading Hours: _____

DAILY ACCOMPLISHMENTS   **FRIDAY 5**

Word Count: _____
Brainstorming Hours: _____
Editing Hours: _____

Marketing Hours: _____
Research Hours: _____
Reading Hours: _____

DAILY ACCOMPLISHMENTS   **SATURDAY 6**

Word Count: _____
Brainstorming Hours: _____
Editing Hours: _____

Marketing Hours: _____
Research Hours: _____
Reading Hours: _____

DAILY ACCOMPLISHMENTS   **SUNDAY 7**

Word Count: _____
Brainstorming Hours: _____
Editing Hours: _____

Marketing Hours: _____
Research Hours: _____
Reading Hours: _____

WEEKLY OVERVIEW

EXERCISE: Take 5-minutes to write something with the 2 words below:

Forest   Highway

Post your exercise on the 4HP Accountable Authors Group on Facebook!

What was your sprint time and top word count?

_____

List a new song you discovered this week:

_____

Favorite food or drink this week:

_____

How did you reward yourself?

_____

What project(s) did you work on?

_____

What are you reading?

_____

What went well this week?

_____

What could improve this week?

_____

_____

_____

TOTAL FOR THE WEEK

Word Count:_____   Marketing Hours:_____
Brainstorming Hours:_____   Research Hours:_____
Editing Hours:_____   Reading Hours:_____

Don't forget to color in your grid!

MAY

The Cheerleader

"*Writing a novel is like driving a car at night. You can only see as far as your headlights, but you can make the whole trip that way.*"

— *E. L. Doctorow*

MAY

THE ARCHITECT

Eliminate passive voice as much as possible.

Passive: This fantasy novel was written by Vanessa.

Active: Vanessa wrote this fantasy novel.

THE RESEARCHER

Hinting to your readers sometimes comes with the descriptors you attach to objects. If I made a point to say a green book from the Renaissance or she ate on bright orange and yellow fiesta plates she inherited from granny, you wouldn't suspect arsenic book covers or radioactive plates! Details matter in your writing as long as you know why.

THE TASKMASTER

"A professional writer is an amateur who did not quit."

~ Richard Bach

You are a professional writer. How do I know this? You bought a skill book to keep you organized and on task. Only a professional would do that.

MAY

WEEK 2

DAILY ACCOMPLISHMENTS	MONDAY 8
WORD COUNT:	MARKETING HOURS:
BRAINSTORMING HOURS:	RESEARCH HOURS:
EDITING HOURS:	READING HOURS:

DAILY ACCOMPLISHMENTS	TUESDAY 9
WORD COUNT:	MARKETING HOURS:
BRAINSTORMING HOURS:	RESEARCH HOURS:
EDITING HOURS:	READING HOURS:

DAILY ACCOMPLISHMENTS	WEDNESDAY 10
WORD COUNT:	MARKETING HOURS:
BRAINSTORMING HOURS:	RESEARCH HOURS:
EDITING HOURS:	READING HOURS:

DAILY ACCOMPLISHMENTS	THURSDAY 11
WORD COUNT:	MARKETING HOURS:
BRAINSTORMING HOURS:	RESEARCH HOURS:
EDITING HOURS:	READING HOURS:

DAILY ACCOMPLISHMENTS	FRIDAY 12
WORD COUNT:	MARKETING HOURS:
BRAINSTORMING HOURS:	RESEARCH HOURS:
EDITING HOURS:	READING HOURS:

DAILY ACCOMPLISHMENTS	SATURDAY 13
WORD COUNT:	MARKETING HOURS:
BRAINSTORMING HOURS:	RESEARCH HOURS:
EDITING HOURS:	READING HOURS:

DAILY ACCOMPLISHMENTS	SUNDAY 14
WORD COUNT:	MARKETING HOURS:
BRAINSTORMING HOURS:	RESEARCH HOURS:
EDITING HOURS:	READING HOURS:

WEEKLY OVERVIEW

Missing   Champagne

What was your sprint time and top word count?

_____

List a new song you discovered this week:

_____

Favorite food or drink this week:

_____

How did you reward yourself?

_____

What project(s) did you work on?

_____

What are you reading?

_____

What went well this week?

_____

What could improve this week?

_____

_____

_____

TOTAL FOR THE WEEK

Word Count:_____   Marketing Hours:_____
Brainstorming Hours:_____   Research Hours:_____
Editing Hours:_____   Reading Hours:_____

Don't forget to color in your grid!

MAY

The Cheerleader

Pay attention to the things that excite you: music, books, movies, hobbies, etc. Use them as inspiration for your stories.

THE ARCHITECT

The original or the remake--which is better?

Defend your position.

THE RESEARCHER

"The art of living is more like wrestling than dancing."
— *Marcus Aurelius*

THE TASKMASTER

You have fans (or will have fans if you haven't been published yet). Even if you can't see them, they're rooting for you--so don't forget to root for yourself!

DAILY ACCOMPLISHMENTS **MONDAY 15**

WORD COUNT:_____ MARKETING HOURS:_____

BRAINSTORMING HOURS:_____ RESEARCH HOURS:_____

EDITING HOURS:_____ READING HOURS:_____

DAILY ACCOMPLISHMENTS **TUESDAY 16**

WORD COUNT:_____ MARKETING HOURS:_____

BRAINSTORMING HOURS:_____ RESEARCH HOURS:_____

EDITING HOURS:_____ READING HOURS:_____

DAILY ACCOMPLISHMENTS **WEDNESDAY 17**

WORD COUNT:_____ MARKETING HOURS:_____

BRAINSTORMING HOURS:_____ RESEARCH HOURS:_____

EDITING HOURS:_____ READING HOURS:_____

DAILY ACCOMPLISHMENTS **THURSDAY 18**

WORD COUNT:_____ MARKETING HOURS:_____

BRAINSTORMING HOURS:_____ RESEARCH HOURS:_____

EDITING HOURS:_____ READING HOURS:_____

DAILY ACCOMPLISHMENTS **FRIDAY 19**

WORD COUNT:_____ MARKETING HOURS:_____

BRAINSTORMING HOURS:_____ RESEARCH HOURS:_____

EDITING HOURS:_____ READING HOURS:_____

DAILY ACCOMPLISHMENTS **SATURDAY 20**

WORD COUNT:_____ MARKETING HOURS:_____

BRAINSTORMING HOURS:_____ RESEARCH HOURS:_____

EDITING HOURS:_____ READING HOURS:_____

DAILY ACCOMPLISHMENTS **SUNDAY 21**

WORD COUNT:_____ MARKETING HOURS:_____

BRAINSTORMING HOURS:_____ RESEARCH HOURS:_____

EDITING HOURS:_____ READING HOURS:_____

MAY

EXERCISE: Take 5-minutes to write something with the 2 words below:

Plaque   Hairbrush

Post your exercise on the 4HP Accountable Authors Group on Facebook!

What was your sprint time and top word count?

_____

List a new song you discovered this week:

_____

Favorite food or drink this week:

_____

How did you reward yourself?

_____

What project(s) did you work on?

_____

What are you reading?

_____

What went well this week?

_____

What could improve this week?

_____

_____

_____

Total for the Week

Word Count:_____   Marketing Hours:_____
Brainstorming Hours:_____   Research Hours:_____
Editing Hours:_____   Reading Hours:_____

Don't forget to color in your grid!

MAY

The Cheerleader

Find a book outside of your comfort zone. Give it a try! (Support your local library!)

THE ARCHITECT

Bio Update: Review your author biography. Tweak for changes.

THE RESEARCHER

Giving a character a skill or job in your world can open opportunities later. During 1880-1881, a carpenter wrote a diary on the underside of floorbards in a chateau where many secrets and confessions about the dark on-goings of his village were recorded including murders and mistresses.

THE TASKMASTER

Increase your word count for next week regardless of your target. Little jumps help get you there faster.

"Must go faster!"

— *Ian Malcolm*

MAY

WEEK 4

DAILY ACCOMPLISHMENTS	MONDAY 22

Word Count: _____
Brainstorming Hours: _____
Editing Hours: _____

Marketing Hours: _____
Research Hours: _____
Reading Hours: _____

DAILY ACCOMPLISHMENTS	TUESDAY 23

Word Count: _____
Brainstorming Hours: _____
Editing Hours: _____

Marketing Hours: _____
Research Hours: _____
Reading Hours: _____

DAILY ACCOMPLISHMENTS	WEDNESDAY 24

Word Count: _____
Brainstorming Hours: _____
Editing Hours: _____

Marketing Hours: _____
Research Hours: _____
Reading Hours: _____

DAILY ACCOMPLISHMENTS	THURSDAY 25

Word Count: _____
Brainstorming Hours: _____
Editing Hours: _____

Marketing Hours: _____
Research Hours: _____
Reading Hours: _____

DAILY ACCOMPLISHMENTS	FRIDAY 26

Word Count: _____
Brainstorming Hours: _____
Editing Hours: _____

Marketing Hours: _____
Research Hours: _____
Reading Hours: _____

DAILY ACCOMPLISHMENTS	SATURDAY 27

Word Count: _____
Brainstorming Hours: _____
Editing Hours: _____

Marketing Hours: _____
Research Hours: _____
Reading Hours: _____

DAILY ACCOMPLISHMENTS	SUNDAY 28

Word Count: _____
Brainstorming Hours: _____
Editing Hours: _____

Marketing Hours: _____
Research Hours: _____
Reading Hours: _____

Weekly Overview

EXERCISE: Take 5-minutes to write something with the 2 words below:

Glorious　　　　Sunshine

Post your exercise on the 4HP Accountable Authors Group on Facebook!

What was your sprint time and top word count?

_____

List a new song you discovered this week:

_____

Favorite food or drink this week:

_____

How did you reward yourself?

_____

What project(s) did you work on?

_____

What are you reading?

_____

What went well this week?

_____

What could improve this week?

_____

_____

_____

MAY

Total for the Week

Word Count:_____　　Marketing Hours:_____
Brainstorming Hours:_____　　Research Hours:_____
Editing Hours:_____　　Reading Hours:_____

Don't forget to color in your grid!

The Cheerleader

"Do not hoard what seems good for a later place in the book, or for another book; give it, give it all, give it now.

— *Annie Dillard*

THE ARCHITECT

World Building is fun because you create all the rules. But don't forget to write them down. Be consistent.

THE RESEARCHER

Can't sleep? Sit down and write! That's exactly what Washington Irving did, the author of *Rip Van Winkle* and *The Legend of Sleepy Hollow*. Insomnia definitely played a part in these stories.

THE TASKMASTER

Are you overediting your work? Stop it. Get the entire story on paper first. Then go back and review what you've done. It's easy to fall into the editing trap. If you need to tag that part with a comment, do it, and then circle back.

MAY

DAILY ACCOMPLISHMENTS   **MONDAY 29**

*WORD COUNT:*_____   *MARKETING HOURS:*_____
*BRAINSTORMING HOURS:*_____   *RESEARCH HOURS:*_____
*EDITING HOURS:*_____   *READING HOURS:*_____

DAILY ACCOMPLISHMENTS   **TUESDAY 30**

*WORD COUNT:*_____   *MARKETING HOURS:*_____
*BRAINSTORMING HOURS:*_____   *RESEARCH HOURS:*_____
*EDITING HOURS:*_____   *READING HOURS:*_____

DAILY ACCOMPLISHMENTS   **WEDNESDAY 31**

*WORD COUNT:*_____   *MARKETING HOURS:*_____
*BRAINSTORMING HOURS:*_____   *RESEARCH HOURS:*_____
*EDITING HOURS:*_____   *READING HOURS:*_____

MAY

THE TASKMASTER

Now is the time to establish your luck for this month. If you do not see a rainbow, create it. You decide on your version of the pot of gold, but be sure to set your goals so that you can succeed. Don't forget that you can join the 4HP Accountable Authors group on Facebook and find people just like you to collaborate with. Good luck, Fellow Author!

WEEKLY OVERVIEW

EXERCISE: Take 5-minutes to write something with the 2 words below:

Mannequin   Whip

Post your exercise on the 4HP Accountable Authors Group on Facebook!

What was your sprint time and top word count?

_____

List a new song you discovered this week:

_____

Favorite food or drink this week:

_____

How did you reward yourself?

_____

What project(s) did you work on?

_____

What are you reading?

_____

What went well this week?

_____

What could improve this week?

_____

_____

_____

TOTAL FOR THE WEEK

Word Count:_____   Marketing Hours:_____
Brainstorming Hours:_____   Research Hours:_____
Editing Hours:_____   Reading Hours:_____

Don't forget to color in your grid!

MAY

MONTHLY ACTIVITY GRID

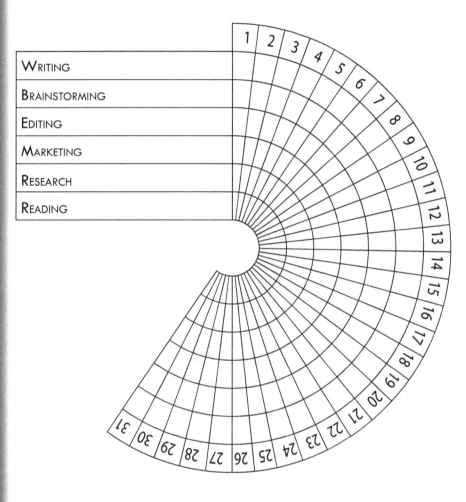

WRITING

BRAINSTORMING

EDITING

MARKETING

RESEARCH

READING

MAY

YOUR AVERAGE WORD COUNT FOR THE MONTH

Total Word Count:_____ Divided by _____ days =_____

TOTAL FOR THE YEAR SO FAR

Word Count:_____   Marketing Hours:_____
Brainstorming Hours:_____   Research Hours:_____
Editing Hours:_____   Reading Hours:_____

JOURNAL

MAY

What was your **top week**?

_____

What made your **top week** successful?

_____

What was your biggest **obstacle**?

_____

How did you **overcome** this? Or could do better next time?

_____

_____

What was your biggest **achievement**?

_____

_____

What **inspired** you most this month?

_____

Did you **discover** a new writing tip or advice this month?

_____

_____

MAY

TOTAL FOR THE MONTH

Word Count:_____   Research Hours:_____
Brainstorming Hours:_____   Reading Hours:_____
Editing Hours:_____
Marketing Hours:_____

TOTAL FOR THE YEAR SO FAR

Word Count:_____   Research Hours:_____
Brainstorming Hours:_____   Reading Hours:_____
Editing Hours:_____
Marketing Hours:_____

Don't forget to color in your grid!

JUNE

You're moving into the halfway mark for the year. Take this time to truly evaluate what is working and not. If you need to change something and you have been putting it off, do it now! You still have time to meet or exceed your goals for this year. Every step counts. We believe in you!

Pride Month & Caribbean-America Heritage Month

June 6 D-Day
Jun 8 Belmont Stakes
June 14 Flag Day

Jun 16 Father's Day
June 19 Juneteenth
Jun 20 June Solstice

WHAT DOES YOUR MONTH LOOK LIKE

Holidays:_____   Weekends:_____

Weekdays:_____   Other:_____

What **project(s)** do you plan on working on?

_____

What **goal** are you aiming to achieve?

_____

What will be your biggest **obstacle** this month?

_____

How will you **overcome** this? Or adjust for this?

_____

What will be your End of the Month **reward**?

_____

GOALS FOR THIS MONTH

Word Count:_____   Marketing Hours:_____

Brainstorming Hours:_____   Research Hours:_____

Editing Hours:_____   Reading Hours:_____

JUNE

JUNE

DAILY ACCOMPLISHMENTS   **THURSDAY 1**

*WORD COUNT:*_____   *MARKETING HOURS:*_____
*BRAINSTORMING HOURS:*_____   *RESEARCH HOURS:*_____
*EDITING HOURS:*_____   *READING HOURS:*_____

DAILY ACCOMPLISHMENTS   **FRIDAY 2**

*WORD COUNT:*_____   *MARKETING HOURS:*_____
*BRAINSTORMING HOURS:*_____   *RESEARCH HOURS:*_____
*EDITING HOURS:*_____   *READING HOURS:*_____

DAILY ACCOMPLISHMENTS   **SATURDAY 3**

*WORD COUNT:*_____   *MARKETING HOURS:*_____
*BRAINSTORMING HOURS:*_____   *RESEARCH HOURS:*_____
*EDITING HOURS:*_____   *READING HOURS:*_____

DAILY ACCOMPLISHMENTS   **SUNDAY 4**

*WORD COUNT:*_____   *MARKETING HOURS:*_____
*BRAINSTORMING HOURS:*_____   *RESEARCH HOURS:*_____
*EDITING HOURS:*_____   *READING HOURS:*_____

DAILY ACCOMPLISHMENTS   **MONDAY 5**

*WORD COUNT:*_____   *MARKETING HOURS:*_____
*BRAINSTORMING HOURS:*_____   *RESEARCH HOURS:*_____
*EDITING HOURS:*_____   *READING HOURS:*_____

DAILY ACCOMPLISHMENTS   **TUESDAY 6**

*WORD COUNT:*_____   *MARKETING HOURS:*_____
*BRAINSTORMING HOURS:*_____   *RESEARCH HOURS:*_____
*EDITING HOURS:*_____   *READING HOURS:*_____

DAILY ACCOMPLISHMENTS   **WEDNESDAY 7**

*WORD COUNT:*_____   *MARKETING HOURS:*_____
*BRAINSTORMING HOURS:*_____   *RESEARCH HOURS:*_____
*EDITING HOURS:*_____   *READING HOURS:*_____

Weekly Overview

EXERCISE: Take 5-minutes to write something with the 2 words below:

Night   Palm

Post your exercise on the 4HP Accountable Authors Group on Facebook!

What was your sprint time and top word count?

_____

List a new song you discovered this week:

_____

Favorite food or drink this week:

_____

How did you reward yourself?

_____

What project(s) did you work on?

_____

What are you reading?

_____

What went well this week?

_____

What could improve this week?

_____

_____

_____

JUNE

Total for the Week

Word Count:_____ Marketing Hours:_____
Brainstorming Hours:_____ Research Hours:_____
Editing Hours:_____ Reading Hours:_____

Don't forget to color in your grid!

The Cheerleader

Record a moment when you last succeeded. You did that? You can totally do this.

JUNE

THE ARCHITECT

Post the blurb of your current project on the 4HP Accountable Authors group on Facebook.

THE RESEARCHER

What's your beverage of choice when you write? The first cup of tea written in history was recorded in Samuel Pepys' diary on September 25, 1660. In his entry, he noted this new tee was a drink from China.

THE TASKMASTER

Are you stuck? Go talk to someone, anyone, about your story. Even if they say nothing useful, talking it out will help you move forward. And who knows, you may find a Muse along the way.

JUNE

DAILY ACCOMPLISHMENTS   **THURSDAY 8**

Word Count: _____   Marketing Hours: _____
Brainstorming Hours: _____   Research Hours: _____
Editing Hours: _____   Reading Hours: _____

DAILY ACCOMPLISHMENTS   **FRIDAY 9**

Word Count: _____   Marketing Hours: _____
Brainstorming Hours: _____   Research Hours: _____
Editing Hours: _____   Reading Hours: _____

DAILY ACCOMPLISHMENTS   **SATURDAY 10**

Word Count: _____   Marketing Hours: _____
Brainstorming Hours: _____   Research Hours: _____
Editing Hours: _____   Reading Hours: _____

DAILY ACCOMPLISHMENTS   **SUNDAY 11**

Word Count: _____   Marketing Hours: _____
Brainstorming Hours: _____   Research Hours: _____
Editing Hours: _____   Reading Hours: _____

DAILY ACCOMPLISHMENTS   **MONDAY 12**

Word Count: _____   Marketing Hours: _____
Brainstorming Hours: _____   Research Hours: _____
Editing Hours: _____   Reading Hours: _____

DAILY ACCOMPLISHMENTS   **TUESDAY 13**

Word Count: _____   Marketing Hours: _____
Brainstorming Hours: _____   Research Hours: _____
Editing Hours: _____   Reading Hours: _____

DAILY ACCOMPLISHMENTS   **WEDNESDAY 14**

Word Count: _____   Marketing Hours: _____
Brainstorming Hours: _____   Research Hours: _____
Editing Hours: _____   Reading Hours: _____

JUNE

Weekly Overview

EXERCISE: Take 5-minutes to write something with the 2 words below:

Taxi   Donut

Post your exercise on the 4HP Accountable Authors Group on Facebook!

What was your sprint time and top word count?

_____

List a new song you discovered this week:

_____

Favorite food or drink this week:

_____

How did you reward yourself?

_____

What project(s) did you work on?

_____

What are you reading?

_____

What went well this week?

_____

What could improve this week?

_____

_____

_____

Total for the Week

Word Count:_____   Marketing Hours:_____
Brainstorming Hours:_____   Research Hours:_____
Editing Hours:_____   Reading Hours:_____

Don't forget to color in your grid!

JUNE

The Cheerleader

Pick a color that describes the mood of your lead character right now! What is it?

THE ARCHITECT

Use comments as notes for your future self. Add thoughts if you are stuck--or to make sure you counted the right number of bullets to reload that gun.

JUNE

THE RESEARCHER

"The superior man is distressed by the limitations of his ability; he is not distressed by the fact that men do not recognize the ability that he has."

— *Confucius*

THE TASKMASTER

Life will happen to you. Acknowledge it, understand it, then move on. Don't let it stop your creativity. Let it fuel you to create more. The world needs your stories.

WEEK 3

DAILY ACCOMPLISHMENTS	**THURSDAY 15**
WORD COUNT:	MARKETING HOURS:
BRAINSTORMING HOURS:	RESEARCH HOURS:
EDITING HOURS:	READING HOURS:

DAILY ACCOMPLISHMENTS	**FRIDAY 16**
WORD COUNT:	MARKETING HOURS:
BRAINSTORMING HOURS:	RESEARCH HOURS:
EDITING HOURS:	READING HOURS:

DAILY ACCOMPLISHMENTS	**SATURDAY 17**
WORD COUNT:	MARKETING HOURS:
BRAINSTORMING HOURS:	RESEARCH HOURS:
EDITING HOURS:	READING HOURS:

DAILY ACCOMPLISHMENTS	**SUNDAY 18**
WORD COUNT:	MARKETING HOURS:
BRAINSTORMING HOURS:	RESEARCH HOURS:
EDITING HOURS:	READING HOURS:

DAILY ACCOMPLISHMENTS	**MONDAY 19**
WORD COUNT:	MARKETING HOURS:
BRAINSTORMING HOURS:	RESEARCH HOURS:
EDITING HOURS:	READING HOURS:

DAILY ACCOMPLISHMENTS	**TUESDAY 20**
WORD COUNT:	MARKETING HOURS:
BRAINSTORMING HOURS:	RESEARCH HOURS:
EDITING HOURS:	READING HOURS:

DAILY ACCOMPLISHMENTS	**WEDNESDAY 21**
WORD COUNT:	MARKETING HOURS:
BRAINSTORMING HOURS:	RESEARCH HOURS:
EDITING HOURS:	READING HOURS:

WEEKLY OVERVIEW

EXERCISE: Take 5-minutes to write something with the 2 words below:

Smoking   Cheese

Post your exercise on the 4HP Accountable Authors Group on Facebook!

What was your sprint time and top word count?

_____

List a new song you discovered this week:

_____

Favorite food or drink this week:

_____

How did you reward yourself?

_____

What project(s) did you work on?

_____

What are you reading?

_____

What went well this week?

_____

What could improve this week?

_____

_____

_____

TOTAL FOR THE WEEK

Word Count:_____   Marketing Hours:_____
Brainstorming Hours:_____   Research Hours:_____
Editing Hours:_____   Reading Hours:_____

Don't forget to color in your grid!

JUNE

The Cheerleader

When was the last time you visited a library? Do you have a library card? If you haven't been in a while, go check it out. Get into the habit of visiting once a month. Don't want to drive? Check out your library's online offerings. You may be pleasantly surprised!

THE ARCHITECT

"All the words I use in my stories can be found in the dictionary—it's just a matter of arranging them into the right sentences."
— *Somerset Maugham*

JUNE

THE RESEARCHER

Life is full of coincidences or near collisions. Sci-fi author H.G. Wells worked as a math teacher before writing his famous *The Time Machine*. What he didn't know was that A.A. Milne was his student, the author who famously wrote *Winnie the Pooh*.

THE TASKMASTER

Spring Cleaning: Set a timer for seven minutes. Write down every project idea in your brain until the alarm rings. Get those thoughts on paper (for later use on a future project). Do this as many times as needed to not interfere with your current project.

JUNE

Daily Accomplishments — Thursday 22

Word Count:_____
Brainstorming Hours:_____
Editing Hours:_____

Marketing Hours:_____
Research Hours:_____
Reading Hours:_____

Daily Accomplishments — Friday 23

Word Count:_____
Brainstorming Hours:_____
Editing Hours:_____

Marketing Hours:_____
Research Hours:_____
Reading Hours:_____

Daily Accomplishments — Saturday 24

Word Count:_____
Brainstorming Hours:_____
Editing Hours:_____

Marketing Hours:_____
Research Hours:_____
Reading Hours:_____

Daily Accomplishments — Sunday 25

Word Count:_____
Brainstorming Hours:_____
Editing Hours:_____

Marketing Hours:_____
Research Hours:_____
Reading Hours:_____

Daily Accomplishments — Monday 26

Word Count:_____
Brainstorming Hours:_____
Editing Hours:_____

Marketing Hours:_____
Research Hours:_____
Reading Hours:_____

Daily Accomplishments — Tuesday 27

Word Count:_____
Brainstorming Hours:_____
Editing Hours:_____

Marketing Hours:_____
Research Hours:_____
Reading Hours:_____

Daily Accomplishments — Wednesday 28

Word Count:_____
Brainstorming Hours:_____
Editing Hours:_____

Marketing Hours:_____
Research Hours:_____
Reading Hours:_____

JUNE

WEEKLY OVERVIEW

EXERCISE: Take 5-minutes to write something with the 2 words below:

Tortilla   Collar

Post your exercise on the 4HP Accountable Authors Group on Facebook!

What was your sprint time and top word count?

_____

List a new song you discovered this week:

_____

Favorite food or drink this week:

_____

How did you reward yourself?

_____

What project(s) did you work on?

_____

What are you reading?

_____

What went well this week?

_____

What could improve this week?

_____

_____

_____

TOTAL FOR THE WEEK

Word Count:_____   Marketing Hours:_____
Brainstorming Hours:_____   Research Hours:_____
Editing Hours:_____   Reading Hours:_____

Don't forget to color in your grid!

The Cheerleader

"Anyone who is going to be a writer knows enough at 15 to write several novels."

— May Sarton

THE ARCHITECT

Best book to movie adaption. Justify it.

THE RESEARCHER

Buy me a castle. Like right now! Man, how on earth did Polish author Henryk Sienkiewicz convince his fellow countrymen to band together in 1900 to buy him the Poznań castle, I don't know. He lived there for a time, and now it's a museum! How did your characters end up living where they are?

THE TASKMASTER

Trust me: what you are writing now will be amazing. Then the next thing you write will be more amazing and this pattern will always continue. You are the best writer you will be in the moment you are in.

JUNE

WEEK 5

DAILY ACCOMPLISHMENTS **THURSDAY 29**

WORD COUNT:_____ MARKETING HOURS:_____
BRAINSTORMING HOURS:_____ RESEARCH HOURS:_____
EDITING HOURS:_____ READING HOURS:_____

DAILY ACCOMPLISHMENTS **FRIDAY 30**

WORD COUNT:_____ MARKETING HOURS:_____
BRAINSTORMING HOURS:_____ RESEARCH HOURS:_____
EDITING HOURS:_____ READING HOURS:_____

The Cheerleader

Stuff You Should Know: You're halfway there! If you were flying to the moon, you'd have traveled 180,000 km by now (assuming the moon is at its closest point to the earth.) June 30th is the 181st day of the year (if it's not a leap year), so that means you would've traveled 994.5 km each day to get where you are right now. That's nearly 619 miles so far--and the Proclaimers only made it 500! Keep going!

EXERCISE: Take 5-minutes to write something with the 2 words below:

Speech   Sticky

Post your exercise on the 4HP Accountable Authors Group on Facebook!

What was your sprint time and top word count?

_____

List a new song you discovered this week:

_____

Favorite food or drink this week:

_____

How did you reward yourself?

_____

What project(s) did you work on?

_____

What are you reading?

_____

What went well this week?

_____

What could improve this week?

_____

_____

_____

TOTAL FOR THE WEEK

Word Count:_____   Marketing Hours:_____
Brainstorming Hours:_____   Research Hours:_____
Editing Hours:_____   Reading Hours:_____

Don't forget to color in your grid!

Monthly Activity Grid

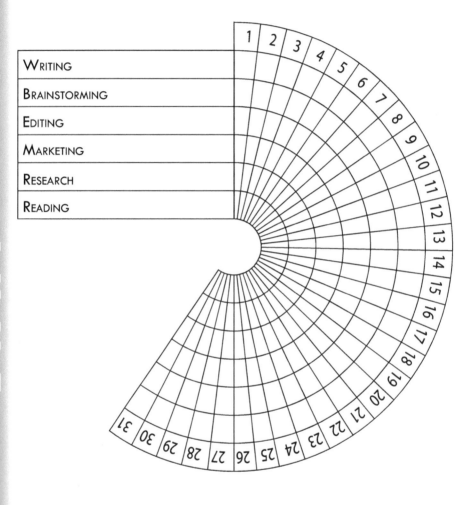

WRITING

BRAINSTORMING

EDITING

MARKETING

RESEARCH

READING

JUNE

Your Average Word Count for the Month

Total Word Count:_____ Divided by _____ days =_____

Total for the Year So Far

Word Count:_____   Marketing Hours:_____
Brainstorming Hours:_____   Research Hours:_____
Editing Hours:_____   Reading Hours:_____

JOURNAL

What was your **top week**?

_____

What made your **top week** successful?

_____

What was your biggest **obstacle**?

_____

How did you **overcome** this? Or could do better next time?

_____

_____

What was your biggest **achievement**?

_____

_____

What **inspired** you most this month?

_____

Did you **discover** a new writing tip or advice this month?

_____

_____

TOTAL FOR THE MONTH

Word Count:_____   Research Hours:_____
Brainstorming Hours:_____   Reading Hours:_____
Editing Hours:_____
Marketing Hours:_____

TOTAL FOR THE YEAR SO FAR

Word Count:_____   Research Hours:_____
Brainstorming Hours:_____   Reading Hours:_____
Editing Hours:_____
Marketing Hours:_____

Don't forget to color in your grid!

JULY

This can be one of the most distracting times of year with fun in the sun. You can always go outside and write. Maybe even find a local coffee shop where the atmosphere is perfect to feel inspired and people-watch at the same time. Again, if you live somewhere where the sun is trying to melt your bones, find a cool hideaway to hang out with your characters!.

July 4 Independence Day　　　*July 16 Rural Transit Day*　　　*July 29 Dog Days of*
July 14 Bastille Day　　　　　*July 28 Parents' Day*　　　　　*Summer Starts*

WHAT DOES YOUR MONTH LOOK LIKE

Holidays:_____　　　Weekends:_____
Weekdays:_____　　　Other:_____

What **project(s)** do you plan on working on?

_____

What **goal** are you aiming to achieve?

_____

What will be your biggest **obstacle** this month?

_____

How will you **overcome** this? Or adjust for this?

_____

What will be your End of the Month **reward**?

_____

GOALS FOR THIS MONTH

Word Count:_____　　　Marketing Hours:_____
Brainstorming Hours:_____　　　Research Hours:_____
Editing Hours:_____　　　Reading Hours:_____

WEEK 1

DAILY ACCOMPLISHMENTS	**SATURDAY 1**
WORD COUNT:	MARKETING HOURS:
BRAINSTORMING HOURS:	RESEARCH HOURS:
EDITING HOURS:	READING HOURS:

DAILY ACCOMPLISHMENTS	**SUNDAY 2**
WORD COUNT:	MARKETING HOURS:
BRAINSTORMING HOURS:	RESEARCH HOURS:
EDITING HOURS:	READING HOURS:

DAILY ACCOMPLISHMENTS	**MONDAY 3**
WORD COUNT:	MARKETING HOURS:
BRAINSTORMING HOURS:	RESEARCH HOURS:
EDITING HOURS:	READING HOURS:

DAILY ACCOMPLISHMENTS	**TUESDAY 4**
WORD COUNT:	MARKETING HOURS:
BRAINSTORMING HOURS:	RESEARCH HOURS:
EDITING HOURS:	READING HOURS:

DAILY ACCOMPLISHMENTS	**WEDNESDAY 5**
WORD COUNT:	MARKETING HOURS:
BRAINSTORMING HOURS:	RESEARCH HOURS:
EDITING HOURS:	READING HOURS:

DAILY ACCOMPLISHMENTS	**THURSDAY 6**
WORD COUNT:	MARKETING HOURS:
BRAINSTORMING HOURS:	RESEARCH HOURS:
EDITING HOURS:	READING HOURS:

DAILY ACCOMPLISHMENTS	**FRIDAY 7**
WORD COUNT:	MARKETING HOURS:
BRAINSTORMING HOURS:	RESEARCH HOURS:
EDITING HOURS:	READING HOURS:

Weekly Overview

What was your sprint time and top word count?

_____

List a new song you discovered this week:

_____

Favorite food or drink this week:

_____

How did you reward yourself?

_____

What project(s) did you work on?

_____

What are you reading?

_____

What went well this week?

_____

What could improve this week?

_____

_____

_____

Total for the Week

Word Count:_____   Marketing Hours:_____
Brainstorming Hours:_____   Research Hours:_____
Editing Hours:_____   Reading Hours:_____

Don't forget to color in your grid!

JULY

The Cheerleader

What's the last book you read in your writing genre? Do you want to write a story like that or not so much? Why?

JULY

THE ARCHITECT

"This sentence has five words. Here are five more words. Five-word sentences are fine. But several together become monotonous. Listen to what is happening. The writing is getting boring. The sound of it drones. It's like a stuck record. The ear demands some variety. Now listen. I vary the sentence length, and I create music. Music. The writing sings. It has a pleasant rhythm, a lilt, a harmony. I use short sentences. And I use sentences of medium length. And sometimes, when I am certain the reader is rested, I will engage him with a sentence of considerable length, a sentence that burns with energy and builds with all the impetus of a crescendo, the role of the drums, the crash of the cymbals—sounds that say listen to this, it is important."

— Gary Provost

THE RESEARCHER

Always carry a lucky charm! It can stop a bullet or arrow and save your life. French Legionnaire soldier Maurice Hamonneau was saved when his copy of Rudyard Kipling's book *Kim* did just that in 1913! What would you characters consider lucky?

THE TASKMASTER

Your work will not be perfect. Nothing is "perfect," so don't wait for that. Instead, keep improving by producing more work. That is the only way.

JULY

WEEK 2

DAILY ACCOMPLISHMENTS	**SATURDAY 8**
Word Count: _____	*Marketing Hours:* _____
Brainstorming Hours: _____	*Research Hours:* _____
Editing Hours: _____	*Reading Hours:* _____

DAILY ACCOMPLISHMENTS	**SUNDAY 9**
Word Count: _____	*Marketing Hours:* _____
Brainstorming Hours: _____	*Research Hours:* _____
Editing Hours: _____	*Reading Hours:* _____

DAILY ACCOMPLISHMENTS	**MONDAY 10**
Word Count: _____	*Marketing Hours:* _____
Brainstorming Hours: _____	*Research Hours:* _____
Editing Hours: _____	*Reading Hours:* _____

DAILY ACCOMPLISHMENTS	**TUESDAY 11**
Word Count: _____	*Marketing Hours:* _____
Brainstorming Hours: _____	*Research Hours:* _____
Editing Hours: _____	*Reading Hours:* _____

DAILY ACCOMPLISHMENTS	**WEDNESDAY 12**
Word Count: _____	*Marketing Hours:* _____
Brainstorming Hours: _____	*Research Hours:* _____
Editing Hours: _____	*Reading Hours:* _____

DAILY ACCOMPLISHMENTS	**THURSDAY 13**
Word Count: _____	*Marketing Hours:* _____
Brainstorming Hours: _____	*Research Hours:* _____
Editing Hours: _____	*Reading Hours:* _____

DAILY ACCOMPLISHMENTS	**FRIDAY 14**
Word Count: _____	*Marketing Hours:* _____
Brainstorming Hours: _____	*Research Hours:* _____
Editing Hours: _____	*Reading Hours:* _____

Weekly Overview

EXERCISE: Take 5-minutes to write something with the 2 words below:

Gloves   Status

Post your exercise on the 4HP Accountable Authors Group on Facebook!

What was your sprint time and top word count?

_____

List a new song you discovered this week:

_____

Favorite food or drink this week:

_____

How did you reward yourself?

_____

What project(s) did you work on?

_____

What are you reading?

_____

What went well this week?

_____

What could improve this week?

_____

_____

_____

Total for the Week

Word Count:_____   Marketing Hours:_____
Brainstorming Hours:_____   Research Hours:_____
Editing Hours:_____   Reading Hours:_____

Don't forget to color in your grid!

JULY

137

The Cheerleader

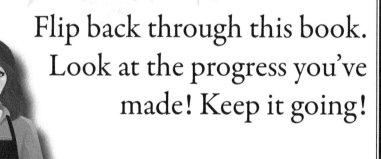

Flip back through this book. Look at the progress you've made! Keep it going!

THE ARCHITECT

Interview Time: Create a list of questions you'd like to ask a character in your project.

THE RESEARCHER

"For a man to conquer himself is the first and noblest of all victories."

— Plato

THE TASKMASTER

"The world is a mess, and I just need to rule it."

~ Dr. Horrible (Dr. Horrible's Sing-a-Long Blog)

It is a mess, and your writing will inspire or provide an escape for your readers. So get a move on, use your hammer, and get it done.

WEEK 3

DAILY ACCOMPLISHMENTS	**SATURDAY 15**
WORD COUNT:	*MARKETING HOURS:*
BRAINSTORMING HOURS:	*RESEARCH HOURS:*
EDITING HOURS:	*READING HOURS:*

DAILY ACCOMPLISHMENTS	**SUNDAY 16**
WORD COUNT:	*MARKETING HOURS:*
BRAINSTORMING HOURS:	*RESEARCH HOURS:*
EDITING HOURS:	*READING HOURS:*

DAILY ACCOMPLISHMENTS	**MONDAY 17**
WORD COUNT:	*MARKETING HOURS:*
BRAINSTORMING HOURS:	*RESEARCH HOURS:*
EDITING HOURS:	*READING HOURS:*

DAILY ACCOMPLISHMENTS	**TUESDAY 18**
WORD COUNT:	*MARKETING HOURS:*
BRAINSTORMING HOURS:	*RESEARCH HOURS:*
EDITING HOURS:	*READING HOURS:*

DAILY ACCOMPLISHMENTS	**WEDNESDAY 19**
WORD COUNT:	*MARKETING HOURS:*
BRAINSTORMING HOURS:	*RESEARCH HOURS:*
EDITING HOURS:	*READING HOURS:*

DAILY ACCOMPLISHMENTS	**THURSDAY 20**
WORD COUNT:	*MARKETING HOURS:*
BRAINSTORMING HOURS:	*RESEARCH HOURS:*
EDITING HOURS:	*READING HOURS:*

DAILY ACCOMPLISHMENTS	**FRIDAY 21**
WORD COUNT:	*MARKETING HOURS:*
BRAINSTORMING HOURS:	*RESEARCH HOURS:*
EDITING HOURS:	*READING HOURS:*

Weekly Overview

EXERCISE: Take 5-minutes to write something with the 2 words below:

Cardboard   Coffee

Post your exercise on the 4HP Accountable Authors Group on Facebook!

What was your sprint time and top word count?

_____

List a new song you discovered this week:

_____

Favorite food or drink this week:

_____

How did you reward yourself?

_____

What project(s) did you work on?

_____

What are you reading?

_____

What went well this week?

_____

What could improve this week?

_____

_____

_____

Total for the Week

Word Count:_____   Marketing Hours:_____
Brainstorming Hours:_____   Research Hours:_____
Editing Hours:_____   Reading Hours:_____

Don't forget to color in your grid!

JULY

The Cheerleader

Coffee vs tea vs wine.
Discuss.

THE ARCHITECT

"People on the outside think there's something magical about writing, that you go up in the attic at midnight and cast the bones and come down in the morning with a story, but it isn't like that. You sit in back of the typewriter and you work, and that's all there is to it."

— Harlan Ellison

JULY

THE RESEARCHER

Okay, what do you keep in your writing desk? Snacks, post-its, or some momento that inspires you when you're stuck? Rumor has it, when Percy Shelley was cremated, his leftover calcified heart was offered to his wife Mary. She accepted it, and rumor has it, she kept it in her writing desk.

THE TASKMASTER

Okay. You are officially halfway through the year. How's it going? If you need to change something, do it. You can reset your goals so they are more reasonable, but you can also challenge yourself to surpass new ones.

JULY

Week 4

DAILY ACCOMPLISHMENTS

SATURDAY 22

Word Count:_____
Brainstorming Hours:_____
Editing Hours:_____

Marketing Hours:_____
Research Hours:_____
Reading Hours:_____

DAILY ACCOMPLISHMENTS

SUNDAY 23

Word Count:_____
Brainstorming Hours:_____
Editing Hours:_____

Marketing Hours:_____
Research Hours:_____
Reading Hours:_____

DAILY ACCOMPLISHMENTS

MONDAY 24

Word Count:_____
Brainstorming Hours:_____
Editing Hours:_____

Marketing Hours:_____
Research Hours:_____
Reading Hours:_____

DAILY ACCOMPLISHMENTS

TUESDAY 25

Word Count:_____
Brainstorming Hours:_____
Editing Hours:_____

Marketing Hours:_____
Research Hours:_____
Reading Hours:_____

DAILY ACCOMPLISHMENTS

WEDNESDAY 26

Word Count:_____
Brainstorming Hours:_____
Editing Hours:_____

Marketing Hours:_____
Research Hours:_____
Reading Hours:_____

DAILY ACCOMPLISHMENTS

THURSDAY 27

Word Count:_____
Brainstorming Hours:_____
Editing Hours:_____

Marketing Hours:_____
Research Hours:_____
Reading Hours:_____

DAILY ACCOMPLISHMENTS

FRIDAY 28

Word Count:_____
Brainstorming Hours:_____
Editing Hours:_____

Marketing Hours:_____
Research Hours:_____
Reading Hours:_____

Weekly Overview

What was your sprint time and top word count?

_____

List a new song you discovered this week:

_____

Favorite food or drink this week:

_____

How did you reward yourself?

_____

What project(s) did you work on?

_____

What are you reading?

_____

What went well this week?

_____

What could improve this week?

_____

_____

_____

Total for the Week

Word Count:_____   Marketing Hours:_____
Brainstorming Hours:_____   Research Hours:_____
Editing Hours:_____   Reading Hours:_____

Don't forget to color in your grid!

JULY

The Cheerleader

"People say, 'What advice do you have for people who want to be writers?' I say, they don't really need advice, they know they want to be writers, and they're gonna do it. Those people who know that they really want to do this and are cut out for it, they know it."

— R.L. Stine

THE ARCHITECT

Use dolls to act out fight scenes (or even sex scenes) to ensure body parts are in the right places.

THE RESEARCHER

Social Media Time: Pay attention to the real world besides your project. Post meaningful content on social media that relates to your writing (share a book, link an article, post a meme, etc.)

THE TASKMASTER

Are you jealous of other writers' accomplishments? Trust me--there are those who are jealous of you. Remember, you're someone else's inspiration; you just might not see it yet.

JULY

DAILY ACCOMPLISHMENTS	SATURDAY 29
WORD COUNT:	MARKETING HOURS:
BRAINSTORMING HOURS:	RESEARCH HOURS:
EDITING HOURS:	READING HOURS:

DAILY ACCOMPLISHMENTS	SUNDAY 30
WORD COUNT:	MARKETING HOURS:
BRAINSTORMING HOURS:	RESEARCH HOURS:
EDITING HOURS:	READING HOURS:

DAILY ACCOMPLISHMENTS	MONDAY 31
WORD COUNT:	MARKETING HOURS:
BRAINSTORMING HOURS:	RESEARCH HOURS:
EDITING HOURS:	READING HOURS:

THE ARCHITECT

What time is it? Time to declare your INDEPENDENCE from bad writing habits or not making enough time for yourself to write. It is easy to get distracted. Make sure you and your project are a priority. Have you been doing your sprints? If not, this is a good time to add them to your schedule. GO GO GO!

JULY

Weekly Overview

What was your sprint time and top word count?

_____

List a new song you discovered this week:

_____

Favorite food or drink this week:

_____

How did you reward yourself?

_____

What project(s) did you work on?

_____

What are you reading?

_____

What went well this week?

_____

What could improve this week?

_____

_____

_____

Total for the Week

Word Count:_____   Marketing Hours:_____
Brainstorming Hours:_____   Research Hours:_____
Editing Hours:_____   Reading Hours:_____

Don't forget to color in your grid!

JULY

149

MONTHLY ACTIVITY GRID

JULY

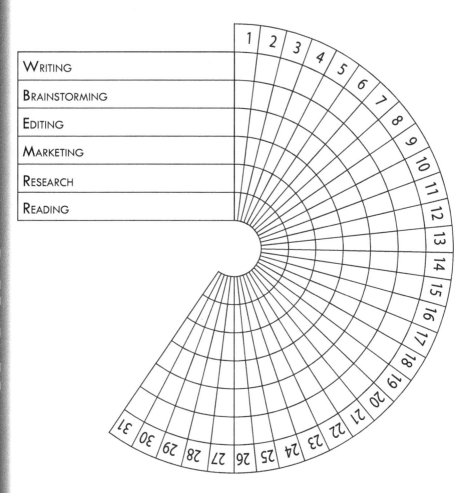

WRITING

BRAINSTORMING

EDITING

MARKETING

RESEARCH

READING

YOUR AVERAGE WORD COUNT FOR THE MONTH

Total Word Count:_____ Divided by _____ days =_____

TOTAL FOR THE YEAR SO FAR

Word Count:_____ Marketing Hours:_____

Brainstorming Hours:_____ Research Hours:_____

Editing Hours:_____ Reading Hours:_____

JOURNAL

What was your **top week**?

_____

What made your **top week** successful?

_____

What was your biggest **obstacle**?

_____

How did you **overcome** this? Or could do better next time?

_____

_____

What was your biggest **achievement**?

_____

_____

What **inspired** you most this month?

_____

Did you **discover** a new writing tip or advice this month?

_____

_____

JULY

TOTAL FOR THE MONTH

Word Count:_____   Research Hours:_____
Brainstorming Hours:_____   Reading Hours:_____
Editing Hours:_____
Marketing Hours:_____

TOTAL FOR THE YEAR SO FAR

Word Count:_____   Research Hours:_____
Brainstorming Hours:_____   Reading Hours:_____
Editing Hours:_____
Marketing Hours:_____

Don't forget to color in your grid!

AUGUST

School is coming soon. Have you thought about some creative writing classes? You do not have to be "in college" to take them. Also, you can find different writing workshops both online and in person. Knowledge is power. Make sure you are constantly learning even more skills as an author. Remember that every time you research something for a scene, that's learning!

Aug 7 Purple Heart Day

Aug 18 National Senior Citizens Day
Aug 19 National Aviation Day

Aug 26 Women's Equality Day

WHAT DOES YOUR MONTH LOOK LIKE

Holidays:_____   Weekends:_____
Weekdays:_____   Other:_____

What **project(s)** do you plan on working on?

_____

What **goal** are you aiming to achieve?

_____

What will be your biggest **obstacle** this month?

_____

How will you **overcome** this? Or adjust for this?

_____

What will be your End of the Month **reward**?

_____

GOALS FOR THIS MONTH

Word Count:_____   Marketing Hours:_____
Brainstorming Hours:_____   Research Hours:_____
Editing Hours:_____   Reading Hours:_____

153

AUGUST

Week 1

DAILY ACCOMPLISHMENTS	**TUESDAY 1**
WORD COUNT:	*MARKETING HOURS:*
BRAINSTORMING HOURS:	*RESEARCH HOURS:*
EDITING HOURS:	*READING HOURS:*

DAILY ACCOMPLISHMENTS	**WEDNESDAY 2**
WORD COUNT:	*MARKETING HOURS:*
BRAINSTORMING HOURS:	*RESEARCH HOURS:*
EDITING HOURS:	*READING HOURS:*

DAILY ACCOMPLISHMENTS	**THURSDAY 3**
WORD COUNT:	*MARKETING HOURS:*
BRAINSTORMING HOURS:	*RESEARCH HOURS:*
EDITING HOURS:	*READING HOURS:*

DAILY ACCOMPLISHMENTS	**FRIDAY 4**
WORD COUNT:	*MARKETING HOURS:*
BRAINSTORMING HOURS:	*RESEARCH HOURS:*
EDITING HOURS:	*READING HOURS:*

DAILY ACCOMPLISHMENTS	**SATURDAY 5**
WORD COUNT:	*MARKETING HOURS:*
BRAINSTORMING HOURS:	*RESEARCH HOURS:*
EDITING HOURS:	*READING HOURS:*

DAILY ACCOMPLISHMENTS	**SUNDAY 6**
WORD COUNT:	*MARKETING HOURS:*
BRAINSTORMING HOURS:	*RESEARCH HOURS:*
EDITING HOURS:	*READING HOURS:*

DAILY ACCOMPLISHMENTS	**MONDAY 7**
WORD COUNT:	*MARKETING HOURS:*
BRAINSTORMING HOURS:	*RESEARCH HOURS:*
EDITING HOURS:	*READING HOURS:*

WEEKLY OVERVIEW

EXERCISE: Take 5-minutes to write something with the 2 words below:

Expectations   Amusement

Post your exercise on the 4HP Accountable Authors Group on Facebook!

What was your sprint time and top word count?

_____

List a new song you discovered this week:

_____

Favorite food or drink this week:

_____

How did you reward yourself?

_____

What project(s) did you work on?

_____

What are you reading?

_____

What went well this week?

_____

What could improve this week?

_____

_____

_____

TOTAL FOR THE WEEK

Word Count:_____   Marketing Hours:_____
Brainstorming Hours:_____   Research Hours:_____
Editing Hours:_____   Reading Hours:_____

Don't forget to color in your grid!

The Cheerleader

Make a list of "Never have I ever" items that you wish to accomplish as a writer.

THE ARCHITECT

"Any man who keeps working is not a failure. He may not be a great writer, but if he applies the old-fashioned virtues of hard, constant labor, he'll eventually make some kind of career for himself as writer."

— *Ray Bradbury*

THE RESEARCHER

Is your character a socialite, a vagabond, or a hermit? For example, Walt Whitman was known to be a traveller with no home (even during the Civil War) while Emily Dickinson stayed in her home alone and tended her garden (she didn't even attend her father's funeral).

THE TASKMASTER

About three things I am absolutely certain:

1) You are awesome!
2) You can reach your goals!
3) Most important, the fans hunger for your words!

Never lose sight of that. (And Edward is a vampire.)

AUGUST

157

WEEK 2

DAILY ACCOMPLISHMENTS | **TUESDAY 8**

WORD COUNT: _____ MARKETING HOURS: _____
BRAINSTORMING HOURS: _____ RESEARCH HOURS: _____
EDITING HOURS: _____ READING HOURS: _____

DAILY ACCOMPLISHMENTS | **WEDNESDAY 9**

WORD COUNT: _____ MARKETING HOURS: _____
BRAINSTORMING HOURS: _____ RESEARCH HOURS: _____
EDITING HOURS: _____ READING HOURS: _____

DAILY ACCOMPLISHMENTS | **THURSDAY 10**

WORD COUNT: _____ MARKETING HOURS: _____
BRAINSTORMING HOURS: _____ RESEARCH HOURS: _____
EDITING HOURS: _____ READING HOURS: _____

DAILY ACCOMPLISHMENTS | **FRIDAY 11**

WORD COUNT: _____ MARKETING HOURS: _____
BRAINSTORMING HOURS: _____ RESEARCH HOURS: _____
EDITING HOURS: _____ READING HOURS: _____

DAILY ACCOMPLISHMENTS | **SATURDAY 12**

WORD COUNT: _____ MARKETING HOURS: _____
BRAINSTORMING HOURS: _____ RESEARCH HOURS: _____
EDITING HOURS: _____ READING HOURS: _____

DAILY ACCOMPLISHMENTS | **SUNDAY 13**

WORD COUNT: _____ MARKETING HOURS: _____
BRAINSTORMING HOURS: _____ RESEARCH HOURS: _____
EDITING HOURS: _____ READING HOURS: _____

DAILY ACCOMPLISHMENTS | **MONDAY 14**

WORD COUNT: _____ MARKETING HOURS: _____
BRAINSTORMING HOURS: _____ RESEARCH HOURS: _____
EDITING HOURS: _____ READING HOURS: _____

WEEKLY OVERVIEW

EXERCISE: Take 5-minutes to write something with the 2 words below:

Chicken   Fluffy

Post your exercise on the 4HP Accountable Authors Group on Facebook!

What was your sprint time and top word count?

_____

List a new song you discovered this week:

_____

Favorite food or drink this week:

_____

How did you reward yourself?

_____

What project(s) did you work on?

_____

What are you reading?

_____

What went well this week?

_____

What could improve this week?

_____

_____

_____

TOTAL FOR THE WEEK

Word Count:_____   Marketing Hours:_____
Brainstorming Hours:_____   Research Hours:_____
Editing Hours:_____   Reading Hours:_____

Don't forget to color in your grid!

AUGUST

The Cheerleader

As Dori says, just keep swimming. Take a moment to breathe. You've got this!

THE ARCHITECT

Find someone who overcame a challenge. Screenshot their picture. Make it the background image on your phone for a day.

AUGUST

THE RESEARCHER

A THIEF! Who in your story steals things and what are they willing to steal? Ernest Hemingway stole the urinal from the bar Sloppy Joe's to put into his home. He is quoted as justifying this with the fact he had "pissed away" enough money there to own it.

THE TASKMASTER

Find your top word count for a day. Then take a day this week and write more than that. Your abilities will amaze you if you stop doubting them.

Week 3

DAILY ACCOMPLISHMENTS   TUESDAY 15

WORD COUNT:_____   MARKETING HOURS:_____
BRAINSTORMING HOURS:_____   RESEARCH HOURS:_____
EDITING HOURS:_____   READING HOURS:_____

DAILY ACCOMPLISHMENTS   WEDNESDAY 16

WORD COUNT:_____   MARKETING HOURS:_____
BRAINSTORMING HOURS:_____   RESEARCH HOURS:_____
EDITING HOURS:_____   READING HOURS:_____

DAILY ACCOMPLISHMENTS   THURSDAY 17

WORD COUNT:_____   MARKETING HOURS:_____
BRAINSTORMING HOURS:_____   RESEARCH HOURS:_____
EDITING HOURS:_____   READING HOURS:_____

DAILY ACCOMPLISHMENTS   FRIDAY 18

WORD COUNT:_____   MARKETING HOURS:_____
BRAINSTORMING HOURS:_____   RESEARCH HOURS:_____
EDITING HOURS:_____   READING HOURS:_____

DAILY ACCOMPLISHMENTS   SATURDAY 19

WORD COUNT:_____   MARKETING HOURS:_____
BRAINSTORMING HOURS:_____   RESEARCH HOURS:_____
EDITING HOURS:_____   READING HOURS:_____

DAILY ACCOMPLISHMENTS   SUNDAY 20

WORD COUNT:_____   MARKETING HOURS:_____
BRAINSTORMING HOURS:_____   RESEARCH HOURS:_____
EDITING HOURS:_____   READING HOURS:_____

DAILY ACCOMPLISHMENTS   MONDAY 21

WORD COUNT:_____   MARKETING HOURS:_____
BRAINSTORMING HOURS:_____   RESEARCH HOURS:_____
EDITING HOURS:_____   READING HOURS:_____

Weekly Overview

Waterfall   Skydiving

Post your exercise on the 4HP Accountable Authors Group on Facebook!

What was your sprint time and top word count?

_____

List a new song you discovered this week:

_____

Favorite food or drink this week:

_____

How did you reward yourself?

_____

What project(s) did you work on?

_____

What are you reading?

_____

What went well this week?

_____

What could improve this week?

_____

_____

_____

Total for the Week

Word Count:_____   Marketing Hours:_____
Brainstorming Hours:_____   Research Hours:_____
Editing Hours:_____   Reading Hours:_____

Don't forget to color in your grid!

AUGUST

163

AUGUST

The Cheerleader

"All we have to decide is what to do with the time that is given to us."
— *Gandalf (Lord of the Rings)*

THE ARCHITECT

Editing got you down? Try editing someone else's work or short story. This is a great way to stretch your muscles without the fog of fretting over your own prose.

THE RESEARCHER

"He that is hard to please may get nothing in the end."

— Aesop

THE TASKMASTER

Every day, do something that scares you. Comfort zones make you complacent. Life is an adventure; don't wait for it to come to you.

AUGUST

165

AUGUST

Daily Accomplishments — Tuesday 22

Word Count: _____
Brainstorming Hours: _____
Editing Hours: _____

Marketing Hours: _____
Research Hours: _____
Reading Hours: _____

Daily Accomplishments — Wednesday 23

Word Count: _____
Brainstorming Hours: _____
Editing Hours: _____

Marketing Hours: _____
Research Hours: _____
Reading Hours: _____

Daily Accomplishments — Thursday 24

Word Count: _____
Brainstorming Hours: _____
Editing Hours: _____

Marketing Hours: _____
Research Hours: _____
Reading Hours: _____

Daily Accomplishments — Friday 25

Word Count: _____
Brainstorming Hours: _____
Editing Hours: _____

Marketing Hours: _____
Research Hours: _____
Reading Hours: _____

Daily Accomplishments — Saturday 26

Word Count: _____
Brainstorming Hours: _____
Editing Hours: _____

Marketing Hours: _____
Research Hours: _____
Reading Hours: _____

Daily Accomplishments — Sunday 27

Word Count: _____
Brainstorming Hours: _____
Editing Hours: _____

Marketing Hours: _____
Research Hours: _____
Reading Hours: _____

Daily Accomplishments — Monday 28

Word Count: _____
Brainstorming Hours: _____
Editing Hours: _____

Marketing Hours: _____
Research Hours: _____
Reading Hours: _____

WEEKLY OVERVIEW

What was your sprint time and top word count?

_____

List a new song you discovered this week:

_____

Favorite food or drink this week:

_____

How did you reward yourself?

_____

What project(s) did you work on?

_____

What are you reading?

_____

What went well this week?

_____

What could improve this week?

_____

_____

_____

TOTAL FOR THE WEEK

Word Count:_____   Marketing Hours:_____
Brainstorming Hours:_____   Research Hours:_____
Editing Hours:_____   Reading Hours:_____

Don't forget to color in your grid!

AUGUST

The Cheerleader

"There are three rules for writing a novel. Unfortunately, no one knows what they are."

— *W. Somerset Maugham*

THE ARCHITECT

Read widely and often. It's a great way to build your internal editor. Start a reading log to track the books you are reading (e-books and audiobooks totally count!).

THE RESEARCHER

You have to start some place. Sometimes our first job leads to the next. The author of *Tarzan*, Edgar Rice Burroughs, was a soldier, railway policeman, door-to-door salesman, and eventually started writing to support his family. Where did your characters begin?

THE TASKMASTER

When was the last time you read your writing out loud? Find an open mic, go, and read. You may be nervous, but hearing your words out loud is a very good idea.

AUGUST

DAILY ACCOMPLISHMENTS		**TUESDAY 29**
WORD COUNT:	MARKETING HOURS:	
BRAINSTORMING HOURS:	RESEARCH HOURS:	
EDITING HOURS:	READING HOURS:	

DAILY ACCOMPLISHMENTS		**WEDNESDAY 30**
WORD COUNT:	MARKETING HOURS:	
BRAINSTORMING HOURS:	RESEARCH HOURS:	
EDITING HOURS:	READING HOURS:	

DAILY ACCOMPLISHMENTS		**THURSDAY 31**
WORD COUNT:	MARKETING HOURS:	
BRAINSTORMING HOURS:	RESEARCH HOURS:	
EDITING HOURS:	READING HOURS:	

AUGUST

THE RESEARCHER

The beginning of fall is fast approaching. Make sure not to fall back on your writing. See what I did there? A pun just for you! How is your writing and publishing knowledge acquisition going? Are you spending time learning some tricks of the trade that you can apply? Good if you are, and you'd better get that going if you are not! This is all about you.

EXERCISE: Take 5-minutes to write something with the 2 words below:

Penguin   Applesauce

Post your exercise on the 4HP Accountable Authors Group on Facebook!

What was your sprint time and top word count?

_____

List a new song you discovered this week:

_____

Favorite food or drink this week:

_____

How did you reward yourself?

_____

What project(s) did you work on?

_____

What are you reading?

_____

What went well this week?

_____

What could improve this week?

_____

_____

_____

TOTAL FOR THE WEEK

Word Count:_____   Marketing Hours:_____
Brainstorming Hours:_____   Research Hours:_____
Editing Hours:_____   Reading Hours:_____

Don't forget to color in your grid!

AUGUST

MONTHLY ACTIVITY GRID

AUGUST

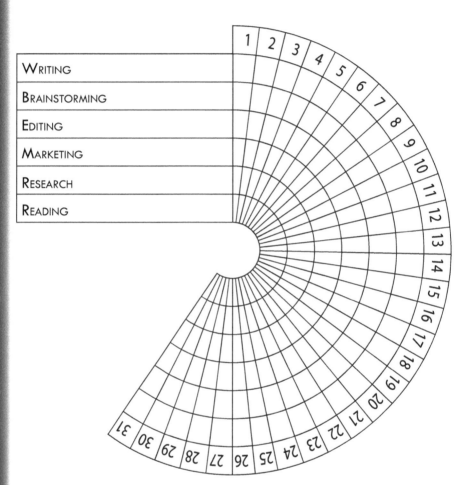

WRITING

BRAINSTORMING

EDITING

MARKETING

RESEARCH

READING

YOUR AVERAGE WORD COUNT FOR THE MONTH

Total Word Count:_____ Divided by _____ days =_____

TOTAL FOR THE YEAR SO FAR

Word Count:_____   Marketing Hours:_____
Brainstorming Hours:_____   Research Hours:_____
Editing Hours:_____   Reading Hours:_____

JOURNAL

What was your **top week**?

_____

What made your **top week** successful?

_____

What was your biggest **obstacle**?

_____

How did you **overcome** this? Or could do better next time?

_____

_____

What was your biggest **achievement**?

_____

_____

What **inspired** you most this month?

_____

Did you **discover** a new writing tip or advice this month?

_____

_____

TOTAL FOR THE MONTH

Word Count:_____   Research Hours:_____
Brainstorming Hours:_____   Reading Hours:_____
Editing Hours:_____
Marketing Hours:_____

TOTAL FOR THE YEAR SO FAR

Word Count:_____   Research Hours:_____
Brainstorming Hours:_____   Reading Hours:_____
Editing Hours:_____
Marketing Hours:_____

Don't forget to color in your grid!

SEPTEMBER

S chool has started again. You might be one of the many hitting the books or helping others to do so. Make sure you do not lose the good habits you formed. Also, this is a great time to find a local writers group. Finding like-minded people in your area or online is one of the most helpful things you can do. Also, don't forget to buy your 2024 Authors Accountability Guide!

Sep 2 Labor Day
Sep 5 The Researcher's Bday
Sep 8 National Grandparents

Sep 11 First Responders Day
Sep 18 Air Force Birthday
Sep 22 Equinox

Sep 28 National Public Lands Day

WHAT DOES YOUR MONTH LOOK LIKE

Holidays:_____   Weekends:_____

Weekdays:_____   Other:_____

What **project(s)** do you plan on working on?

_____

What **goal** are you aiming to achieve?

_____

What will be your biggest **obstacle** this month?

_____

How will you **overcome** this? Or adjust for this?

_____

What will be your End of the Month **reward**?

_____

GOALS FOR THIS MONTH

Word Count:_____   Marketing Hours:_____

Brainstorming Hours:_____   Research Hours:_____

Editing Hours:_____   Reading Hours:_____

SEPTEMBER

WEEK 1

SEPTEMBER

DAILY ACCOMPLISHMENTS   **FRIDAY 1**

*WORD COUNT:*_____   *MARKETING HOURS:*_____
*BRAINSTORMING HOURS:*_____   *RESEARCH HOURS:*_____
*EDITING HOURS:*_____   *READING HOURS:*_____

DAILY ACCOMPLISHMENTS   **SATURDAY 2**

*WORD COUNT:*_____   *MARKETING HOURS:*_____
*BRAINSTORMING HOURS:*_____   *RESEARCH HOURS:*_____
*EDITING HOURS:*_____   *READING HOURS:*_____

DAILY ACCOMPLISHMENTS   **SUNDAY 3**

*WORD COUNT:*_____   *MARKETING HOURS:*_____
*BRAINSTORMING HOURS:*_____   *RESEARCH HOURS:*_____
*EDITING HOURS:*_____   *READING HOURS:*_____

DAILY ACCOMPLISHMENTS   **MONDAY 4**

*WORD COUNT:*_____   *MARKETING HOURS:*_____
*BRAINSTORMING HOURS:*_____   *RESEARCH HOURS:*_____
*EDITING HOURS:*_____   *READING HOURS:*_____

DAILY ACCOMPLISHMENTS   **TUESDAY 5**

*WORD COUNT:*_____   *MARKETING HOURS:*_____
*BRAINSTORMING HOURS:*_____   *RESEARCH HOURS:*_____
*EDITING HOURS:*_____   *READING HOURS:*_____

DAILY ACCOMPLISHMENTS   **WEDNESDAY 6**

*WORD COUNT:*_____   *MARKETING HOURS:*_____
*BRAINSTORMING HOURS:*_____   *RESEARCH HOURS:*_____
*EDITING HOURS:*_____   *READING HOURS:*_____

DAILY ACCOMPLISHMENTS   **THURSDAY 7**

*WORD COUNT:*_____   *MARKETING HOURS:*_____
*BRAINSTORMING HOURS:*_____   *RESEARCH HOURS:*_____
*EDITING HOURS:*_____   *READING HOURS:*_____

WEEKLY OVERVIEW

EXERCISE: Take 5-minutes to write something with the 2 words below:

Beans   Note

Post your exercise on the 4HP Accountable Authors Group on Facebook!

What was your sprint time and top word count?

_____

List a new song you discovered this week:

_____

Favorite food or drink this week:

_____

How did you reward yourself?

_____

What project(s) did you work on?

_____

What are you reading?

_____

What went well this week?

_____

What could improve this week?

_____

_____

_____

TOTAL FOR THE WEEK

Word Count:_____   Marketing Hours:_____
Brainstorming Hours:_____   Research Hours:_____
Editing Hours:_____   Reading Hours:_____

Don't forget to color in your grid!

SEPTEMBER

The Cheerleader

Do you keep notes about your characters? Make sure to track details about them and their relationships. I know it's fresh right now, but you probably won't remember this detail three books from now.

THE ARCHITECT

Plot Holes Everywhere: What plot issues are you struggling with right now? Jot down possible stopgaps to explain the events.

THE RESEARCHER

In your world, what can be taken or given away? Who knew Robert Louis Stevenson, author of *Treasure Island*, gave away his birthday to a little girl who had hers on Christmas Day? Imagine the impact this made on the girl!

THE TASKMASTER

What's your worst fear as a writer? Write it down on paper. Then rip it to shreds or burn it. Good-- you're done with that now. Move forward.

SEPTEMBER

179

DAILY ACCOMPLISHMENTS   **FRIDAY 8**

WORD COUNT:_____   MARKETING HOURS:_____
BRAINSTORMING HOURS:_____   RESEARCH HOURS:_____
EDITING HOURS:_____   READING HOURS:_____

DAILY ACCOMPLISHMENTS   **SATURDAY 9**

WORD COUNT:_____   MARKETING HOURS:_____
BRAINSTORMING HOURS:_____   RESEARCH HOURS:_____
EDITING HOURS:_____   READING HOURS:_____

DAILY ACCOMPLISHMENTS   **SUNDAY 10**

WORD COUNT:_____   MARKETING HOURS:_____
BRAINSTORMING HOURS:_____   RESEARCH HOURS:_____
EDITING HOURS:_____   READING HOURS:_____

DAILY ACCOMPLISHMENTS   **MONDAY 11**

WORD COUNT:_____   MARKETING HOURS:_____
BRAINSTORMING HOURS:_____   RESEARCH HOURS:_____
EDITING HOURS:_____   READING HOURS:_____

DAILY ACCOMPLISHMENTS   **TUESDAY 12**

WORD COUNT:_____   MARKETING HOURS:_____
BRAINSTORMING HOURS:_____   RESEARCH HOURS:_____
EDITING HOURS:_____   READING HOURS:_____

DAILY ACCOMPLISHMENTS   **WEDNESDAY 13**

WORD COUNT:_____   MARKETING HOURS:_____
BRAINSTORMING HOURS:_____   RESEARCH HOURS:_____
EDITING HOURS:_____   READING HOURS:_____

DAILY ACCOMPLISHMENTS   **THURSDAY 14**

WORD COUNT:_____   MARKETING HOURS:_____
BRAINSTORMING HOURS:_____   RESEARCH HOURS:_____
EDITING HOURS:_____   READING HOURS:_____

S E P T E M B E R

WEEKLY OVERVIEW

EXERCISE: Take 5-minutes to write something with the 2 words below:

Joke   Social

Post your exercise on the 4HP Accountable Authors Group on Facebook!

What was your sprint time and top word count?

_____

List a new song you discovered this week:

_____

Favorite food or drink this week:

_____

How did you reward yourself?

_____

What project(s) did you work on?

_____

What are you reading?

_____

What went well this week?

_____

What could improve this week?

_____

_____

_____

TOTAL FOR THE WEEK

Word Count:_____   Marketing Hours:_____
Brainstorming Hours:_____   Research Hours:_____
Editing Hours:_____   Reading Hours:_____

Don't forget to color in your grid!

SEPTEMBER

The Cheerleader

Write a piece of flash fiction (1000 words or less) and post it on your social media. Put the title here.

THE ARCHITECT

Vocab Building Time: Learn five new words. Flip through a dictionary, scroll through an online dictionary-- whatever works for you.

SEPTEMBER

THE RESEARCHER

"Enough is as good as a feast."
— Sir Thomas Malory

THE TASKMASTER

Remember, you will find that people like to share stories. If you're writing about someone from a different background or place, then find someone from there and ask questions. This will make your characters feel more real.

SEPTEMBER

WEEK 3

DAILY ACCOMPLISHMENTS   **FRIDAY 15**

WORD COUNT:_____   MARKETING HOURS:_____
BRAINSTORMING HOURS:_____   RESEARCH HOURS:_____
EDITING HOURS:_____   READING HOURS:_____

DAILY ACCOMPLISHMENTS   **SATURDAY 16**

WORD COUNT:_____   MARKETING HOURS:_____
BRAINSTORMING HOURS:_____   RESEARCH HOURS:_____
EDITING HOURS:_____   READING HOURS:_____

DAILY ACCOMPLISHMENTS   **SUNDAY 17**

WORD COUNT:_____   MARKETING HOURS:_____
BRAINSTORMING HOURS:_____   RESEARCH HOURS:_____
EDITING HOURS:_____   READING HOURS:_____

DAILY ACCOMPLISHMENTS   **MONDAY 18**

WORD COUNT:_____   MARKETING HOURS:_____
BRAINSTORMING HOURS:_____   RESEARCH HOURS:_____
EDITING HOURS:_____   READING HOURS:_____

DAILY ACCOMPLISHMENTS   **TUESDAY 19**

WORD COUNT:_____   MARKETING HOURS:_____
BRAINSTORMING HOURS:_____   RESEARCH HOURS:_____
EDITING HOURS:_____   READING HOURS:_____

DAILY ACCOMPLISHMENTS   **WEDNESDAY 20**

WORD COUNT:_____   MARKETING HOURS:_____
BRAINSTORMING HOURS:_____   RESEARCH HOURS:_____
EDITING HOURS:_____   READING HOURS:_____

DAILY ACCOMPLISHMENTS   **THURSDAY 21**

WORD COUNT:_____   MARKETING HOURS:_____
BRAINSTORMING HOURS:_____   RESEARCH HOURS:_____
EDITING HOURS:_____   READING HOURS:_____

Weekly Overview

EXERCISE: Take 5-minutes to write something with the 2 words below:

Haircut   Dress

Post your exercise on the 4HP Accountable Authors Group on Facebook!

What was your sprint time and top word count?

_____

List a new song you discovered this week:

_____

Favorite food or drink this week:

_____

How did you reward yourself?

_____

What project(s) did you work on?

_____

What are you reading?

_____

What went well this week?

_____

What could improve this week?

_____

_____

_____

Total for the Week

Word Count:_____   Marketing Hours:_____
Brainstorming Hours:_____   Research Hours:_____
Editing Hours:_____   Reading Hours:_____

Don't forget to color in your grid!

SEPTEMBER

The Cheerleader

Don't wait. The timing will never be just right. The best time is right now. The next best time is right now.

THE ARCHITECT

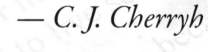

"It is perfectly okay to write garbage— as long as you edit brilliantly."
— *C. J. Cherryh*

SEPTEMBER

THE RESEARCHER

What happens after death in your story? I mean, if you can find a video on the life-size android of the sci-fi author Philip K. Dick, anything is possible, right? Unfortunately, its head disappeared while flying from Dallas to San Franciso when he was accidentally left in the overhead compartment. What things do you leave behind after life? I wonder...

THE TASKMASTER

Do you have your business cards as a writer yet? If you don't, get them now! Take them everywhere--and I do mean everywhere! You will be suprised how many times you hand them out.

SEPTEMBER

SEPTEMBER

DAILY ACCOMPLISHMENTS   FRIDAY 22

WORD COUNT:_____   MARKETING HOURS:_____
BRAINSTORMING HOURS:_____ RESEARCH HOURS:_____
EDITING HOURS:_____   READING HOURS:_____

DAILY ACCOMPLISHMENTS   SATURDAY 23

WORD COUNT:_____   MARKETING HOURS:_____
BRAINSTORMING HOURS:_____ RESEARCH HOURS:_____
EDITING HOURS:_____   READING HOURS:_____

DAILY ACCOMPLISHMENTS   SUNDAY 24

WORD COUNT:_____   MARKETING HOURS:_____
BRAINSTORMING HOURS:_____ RESEARCH HOURS:_____
EDITING HOURS:_____   READING HOURS:_____

DAILY ACCOMPLISHMENTS   MONDAY 25

WORD COUNT:_____   MARKETING HOURS:_____
BRAINSTORMING HOURS:_____ RESEARCH HOURS:_____
EDITING HOURS:_____   READING HOURS:_____

DAILY ACCOMPLISHMENTS   TUESDAY 26

WORD COUNT:_____   MARKETING HOURS:_____
BRAINSTORMING HOURS:_____ RESEARCH HOURS:_____
EDITING HOURS:_____   READING HOURS:_____

DAILY ACCOMPLISHMENTS   WEDNESDAY 27

WORD COUNT:_____   MARKETING HOURS:_____
BRAINSTORMING HOURS:_____ RESEARCH HOURS:_____
EDITING HOURS:_____   READING HOURS:_____

DAILY ACCOMPLISHMENTS   THURSDAY 28

WORD COUNT:_____   MARKETING HOURS:_____
BRAINSTORMING HOURS:_____ RESEARCH HOURS:_____
EDITING HOURS:_____   READING HOURS:_____

WEEKLY OVERVIEW

EXERCISE: Take 5-minutes to write something with the 2 words below:

Boots   Tires

Post your exercise on the 4HP Accountable Authors Group on Facebook!

What was your sprint time and top word count?

_____

List a new song you discovered this week:

_____

Favorite food or drink this week:

_____

How did you reward yourself?

_____

What project(s) did you work on?

_____

What are you reading?

_____

What went well this week?

_____

What could improve this week?

_____

_____

_____

TOTAL FOR THE WEEK

Word Count:_____   Marketing Hours:_____
Brainstorming Hours:_____   Research Hours:_____
Editing Hours:_____   Reading Hours:_____

Don't forget to color in your grid!

SEPTEMBER

The Cheerleader

"Every secret of a writer's soul, every experience of his life, every quality of his mind, is written large in his works."

— *Virginia Woolf*

THE ARCHITECT

Worst book to movie adaptation. Eviscerate it.

THE RESEARCHER

Famous last words can be quite revealing about a character. Playwright Eugene O'Neill was quoted, "I knew it. I knew it. Born in a hotel room – and God damn it – died in a hotel room." What dialogue has impact in your story that reveals emotion and backstory as much as this?

THE TASKMASTER

Don't "try" to write. Just write! It's that simple. Even if you have to put aside your current project, write a piece of flash fiction, or do another exercise--just continue to be creative.

SEPTEMBER

DAILY ACCOMPLISHMENTS	**FRIDAY 29**
WORD COUNT:	*MARKETING HOURS:*
BRAINSTORMING HOURS:	*RESEARCH HOURS:*
EDITING HOURS:	*READING HOURS:*

DAILY ACCOMPLISHMENTS	**SATURDAY 30**
WORD COUNT:	*MARKETING HOURS:*
BRAINSTORMING HOURS:	*RESEARCH HOURS:*
EDITING HOURS:	*READING HOURS:*

THE TASKMASTER

We are nearing the end of the third quarter. Time can run away. It is the only commodity you can never get back. Make the most of it! As we are nearing crunch time (*aka the end of the year*), make sure you are taking time for you: a hike in the woods, a bike ride, a beer with a friend, or a bubble-bath. Keeping yourself in mind will make the journey that much easier.

SEPTEMBER

Weekly Overview

EXERCISE: Take 5-minutes to write something with the 2 words below:

Translation   Mushroom

Post your exercise on the 4HP Accountable Authors Group on Facebook!

What was your sprint time and top word count?

_____

List a new song you discovered this week:

_____

Favorite food or drink this week:

_____

How did you reward yourself?

_____

What project(s) did you work on?

_____

What are you reading?

_____

What went well this week?

_____

What could improve this week?

_____

_____

_____

_____

Total for the Week

Word Count:_____   Marketing Hours:_____
Brainstorming Hours:_____   Research Hours:_____
Editing Hours:_____   Reading Hours:_____

Don't forget to color in your grid!

SEPTEMBER

Monthly Activity Grid

S E P T E M B E R

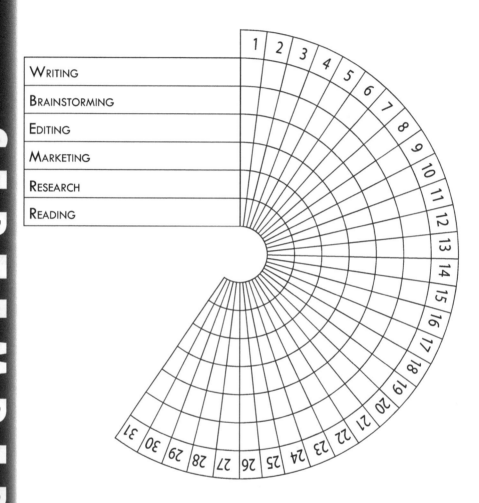

WRITING

BRAINSTORMING

EDITING

MARKETING

RESEARCH

READING

Your Average Word Count for the Month

Total Word Count:_____ Divided by _____ days = _____

Total for the Year So Far

Word Count:_____   Marketing Hours:_____

Brainstorming Hours:_____   Research Hours:_____

Editing Hours:_____   Reading Hours:_____

JOURNAL

What was your **top week**?

_____

What made your **top week** successful?

_____

What was your biggest **obstacle**?

_____

How did you **overcome** this? Or could do better next time?

_____

_____

What was your biggest **achievement**?

_____

_____

What **inspired** you most this month?

_____

Did you **discover** a new writing tip or advice this month?

_____

_____

TOTAL FOR THE MONTH

Word Count:_____   Research Hours:_____
Brainstorming Hours:_____   Reading Hours:_____
Editing Hours:_____
Marketing Hours:_____

TOTAL FOR THE YEAR SO FAR

Word Count:_____   Research Hours:_____
Brainstorming Hours:_____   Reading Hours:_____
Editing Hours:_____
Marketing Hours:_____

S E P T E M B E R

Don't forget to color in your grid!

OCTOBER

I t is the spookiest month of the year--the Muses' favorite holiday: Halloween! Besides wearing costumes and trick-or-treating, they say this is the time when the veil between worlds is the thinnest. This is the time to realize you only have three months left of 2023--and that NANO is one month away. Time to get prepared, grab a pumpkin-spiced latte and as much candy corn as you can stomach, and keep your inner demons at bay.

Oct 5 World Teachers' Day   *Oct 14 Columbus Day*   *Oct 19 Sweetest Day*
Oct 13 Navy Birthday   *Oct 16 Boss' Day*   *Oct 31 Halloween*

WHAT DOES YOUR MONTH LOOK LIKE

Holidays:_____   Weekends:_____
Weekdays:_____   Other:_____

What **project(s)** do you plan on working on?

_____

What **goal** are you aiming to achieve?

_____

What will be your biggest **obstacle** this month?

_____

How will you **overcome** this? Or adjust for this?

_____

What will be your End of the Month **reward**?

_____

GOALS FOR THIS MONTH

Word Count:_____   Marketing Hours:_____
Brainstorming Hours:_____   Research Hours:_____
Editing Hours:_____   Reading Hours:_____

OCTOBER

DAILY ACCOMPLISHMENTS   SUNDAY 1

WORD COUNT:_____   MARKETING HOURS:_____

BRAINSTORMING HOURS:_____   RESEARCH HOURS:_____

EDITING HOURS:_____   READING HOURS:_____

DAILY ACCOMPLISHMENTS   MONDAY 2

WORD COUNT:_____   MARKETING HOURS:_____

BRAINSTORMING HOURS:_____   RESEARCH HOURS:_____

EDITING HOURS:_____   READING HOURS:_____

DAILY ACCOMPLISHMENTS   TUESDAY 3

WORD COUNT:_____   MARKETING HOURS:_____

BRAINSTORMING HOURS:_____   RESEARCH HOURS:_____

EDITING HOURS:_____   READING HOURS:_____

DAILY ACCOMPLISHMENTS   WEDNESDAY 4

WORD COUNT:_____   MARKETING HOURS:_____

BRAINSTORMING HOURS:_____   RESEARCH HOURS:_____

EDITING HOURS:_____   READING HOURS:_____

DAILY ACCOMPLISHMENTS   THURSDAY 5

WORD COUNT:_____   MARKETING HOURS:_____

BRAINSTORMING HOURS:_____   RESEARCH HOURS:_____

EDITING HOURS:_____   READING HOURS:_____

DAILY ACCOMPLISHMENTS   FRIDAY 6

WORD COUNT:_____   MARKETING HOURS:_____

BRAINSTORMING HOURS:_____   RESEARCH HOURS:_____

EDITING HOURS:_____   READING HOURS:_____

DAILY ACCOMPLISHMENTS   SATURDAY 7

WORD COUNT:_____   MARKETING HOURS:_____

BRAINSTORMING HOURS:_____   RESEARCH HOURS:_____

EDITING HOURS:_____   READING HOURS:_____

Weekly Overview

Purse　　　　　Mask

Post your exercise on the 4HP Accountable Authors Group on Facebook!

What was your sprint time and top word count?

_____

List a new song you discovered this week:

_____

Favorite food or drink this week:

_____

How did you reward yourself?

_____

What project(s) did you work on?

_____

What are you reading?

_____

What went well this week?

_____

What could improve this week?

_____

_____

_____

Total for the Week

Word Count:_____　　Marketing Hours:_____
Brainstorming Hours:_____　　Research Hours:_____
Editing Hours:_____　　Reading Hours:_____

Don't forget to color in your grid!

OCTOBER

199

The Cheerleader

Write at a different time once this week.

How did it go?

THE ARCHITECT

Search for filter words: "She saw, she heard, she noticed, etc." Then try to eliminate them as much as you can.

OCTOBER

THE RESEARCHER

"Do not say a little in many words but a great deal in few."

— *Pythagoras*

THE TASKMASTER

If you're wondering if you're writing enough, the answer is no. Your fans want more from you. Give it to them.

OCTOBER

DAILY ACCOMPLISHMENTS   **SUNDAY 8**

*WORD COUNT:*_____   *MARKETING HOURS:*_____
*BRAINSTORMING HOURS:*_____   *RESEARCH HOURS:*_____
*EDITING HOURS:*_____   *READING HOURS:*_____

DAILY ACCOMPLISHMENTS   **MONDAY 9**

*WORD COUNT:*_____   *MARKETING HOURS:*_____
*BRAINSTORMING HOURS:*_____   *RESEARCH HOURS:*_____
*EDITING HOURS:*_____   *READING HOURS:*_____

DAILY ACCOMPLISHMENTS   **TUESDAY 10**

*WORD COUNT:*_____   *MARKETING HOURS:*_____
*BRAINSTORMING HOURS:*_____   *RESEARCH HOURS:*_____
*EDITING HOURS:*_____   *READING HOURS:*_____

DAILY ACCOMPLISHMENTS   **WEDNESDAY 11**

*WORD COUNT:*_____   *MARKETING HOURS:*_____
*BRAINSTORMING HOURS:*_____   *RESEARCH HOURS:*_____
*EDITING HOURS:*_____   *READING HOURS:*_____

DAILY ACCOMPLISHMENTS   **THURSDAY 12**

*WORD COUNT:*_____   *MARKETING HOURS:*_____
*BRAINSTORMING HOURS:*_____   *RESEARCH HOURS:*_____
*EDITING HOURS:*_____   *READING HOURS:*_____

DAILY ACCOMPLISHMENTS   **FRIDAY 13**

*WORD COUNT:*_____   *MARKETING HOURS:*_____
*BRAINSTORMING HOURS:*_____   *RESEARCH HOURS:*_____
*EDITING HOURS:*_____   *READING HOURS:*_____

DAILY ACCOMPLISHMENTS   **SATURDAY 14**

*WORD COUNT:*_____   *MARKETING HOURS:*_____
*BRAINSTORMING HOURS:*_____   *RESEARCH HOURS:*_____
*EDITING HOURS:*_____   *READING HOURS:*_____

OCTOBER

WEEKLY OVERVIEW

EXERCISE: Take 5-minutes to write something with the 2 words below:

Stuffed   Blanket

Post your exercise on the 4HP Accountable Authors Group on Facebook!

What was your sprint time and top word count?

_____

List a new song you discovered this week:

_____

Favorite food or drink this week:

_____

How did you reward yourself?

_____

What project(s) did you work on?

_____

What are you reading?

_____

What went well this week?

_____

What could improve this week?

_____

_____

_____

TOTAL FOR THE WEEK

Word Count:_____   Marketing Hours:_____
Brainstorming Hours:_____   Research Hours:_____
Editing Hours:_____   Reading Hours:_____

Don't forget to color in your grid!

OCTOBER

The Cheerleader

"Look! I have one job on this ship. It's stupid, but I'm going to do it."

— *Gwen DeMarco*
(Galaxy Quest)

Nothing you write is stupid. The act of writing has meaning and value. Do your job and get those words on the page!

THE ARCHITECT

Switch gears and work on a different project this week. How did it go?

THE RESEARCHER

Writing sprints and building strong habits or routines can make a difference. Victorian novelist Anthony Trollope woke at 5:30 am, drank his coffee, and wrote for three hours before going to work. It's said he could write 250 words in 15 minutes; most writers today can type at that rate.

THE TASKMASTER

Do you believe your writing won't be appreciated by others? Well, you're wrong. If there's an audience for dinosaur romance, there are people ready to hear your story.

OCTOBER

WEEK 3

DAILY ACCOMPLISHMENTS **SUNDAY 15**

WORD COUNT:_____
BRAINSTORMING HOURS:_____
EDITING HOURS:_____

MARKETING HOURS:_____
RESEARCH HOURS:_____
READING HOURS:_____

DAILY ACCOMPLISHMENTS **MONDAY 16**

WORD COUNT:_____
BRAINSTORMING HOURS:_____
EDITING HOURS:_____

MARKETING HOURS:_____
RESEARCH HOURS:_____
READING HOURS:_____

DAILY ACCOMPLISHMENTS **TUESDAY 17**

WORD COUNT:_____
BRAINSTORMING HOURS:_____
EDITING HOURS:_____

MARKETING HOURS:_____
RESEARCH HOURS:_____
READING HOURS:_____

DAILY ACCOMPLISHMENTS **WEDNESDAY 18**

WORD COUNT:_____
BRAINSTORMING HOURS:_____
EDITING HOURS:_____

MARKETING HOURS:_____
RESEARCH HOURS:_____
READING HOURS:_____

DAILY ACCOMPLISHMENTS **THURSDAY 19**

WORD COUNT:_____
BRAINSTORMING HOURS:_____
EDITING HOURS:_____

MARKETING HOURS:_____
RESEARCH HOURS:_____
READING HOURS:_____

DAILY ACCOMPLISHMENTS **FRIDAY 20**

WORD COUNT:_____
BRAINSTORMING HOURS:_____
EDITING HOURS:_____

MARKETING HOURS:_____
RESEARCH HOURS:_____
READING HOURS:_____

DAILY ACCOMPLISHMENTS **SATURDAY 21**

WORD COUNT:_____
BRAINSTORMING HOURS:_____
EDITING HOURS:_____

MARKETING HOURS:_____
RESEARCH HOURS:_____
READING HOURS:_____

OCTOBER

Weekly Overview

EXERCISE: Take 5-minutes to write something with the 2 words below:

Fringe   Comrade

Post your exercise on the 4HP Accountable Authors Group on Facebook!

What was your sprint time and top word count?

_____

List a new song you discovered this week:

_____

Favorite food or drink this week:

_____

How did you reward yourself?

_____

What project(s) did you work on?

_____

What are you reading?

_____

What went well this week?

_____

What could improve this week?

_____

_____

_____

TOTAL FOR THE WEEK

Word Count:_____   Marketing Hours:_____
Brainstorming Hours:_____   Research Hours:_____
Editing Hours:_____   Reading Hours:_____

Don't forget to color in your grid!

The Cheerleader

Build a system! Create a money scheme, craft a calendar, draw a family tree, describe the intricacies of how a town operates, or anything else that will maintain your writing focus.

THE ARCHITECT

Interview Time: What questions would a reporter ask your hero, villain, or main character? Is it related to an event that happens in the book? Or a decision they made? Now share it!

OCTOBER

THE RESEARCHER

How does the story end? Which ending is the right one? Sometimes you need to try writing them all! Yasunari Kawabata wrote dozens of conclusions for his masterpiece *Snow Country*. This led him to become the first Japanese Nobel Prize winner in literature in 1968.

THE TASKMASTER

"The worst enemy to creativity is self-doubt."

— *Sylvia Plath*

Never doubt what you can accomplish or if it's good enough. You're doing it, and it is fantastic!

OCTOBER

209

WEEK 4

OCTOBER (vertical, left margin)

DAILY ACCOMPLISHMENTS	SUNDAY 22
WORD COUNT:	MARKETING HOURS:
BRAINSTORMING HOURS:	RESEARCH HOURS:
EDITING HOURS:	READING HOURS:

DAILY ACCOMPLISHMENTS	MONDAY 23
WORD COUNT:	MARKETING HOURS:
BRAINSTORMING HOURS:	RESEARCH HOURS:
EDITING HOURS:	READING HOURS:

DAILY ACCOMPLISHMENTS	TUESDAY 24
WORD COUNT:	MARKETING HOURS:
BRAINSTORMING HOURS:	RESEARCH HOURS:
EDITING HOURS:	READING HOURS:

DAILY ACCOMPLISHMENTS	WEDNESDAY 25
WORD COUNT:	MARKETING HOURS:
BRAINSTORMING HOURS:	RESEARCH HOURS:
EDITING HOURS:	READING HOURS:

DAILY ACCOMPLISHMENTS	THURSDAY 26
WORD COUNT:	MARKETING HOURS:
BRAINSTORMING HOURS:	RESEARCH HOURS:
EDITING HOURS:	READING HOURS:

DAILY ACCOMPLISHMENTS	FRIDAY 27
WORD COUNT:	MARKETING HOURS:
BRAINSTORMING HOURS:	RESEARCH HOURS:
EDITING HOURS:	READING HOURS:

DAILY ACCOMPLISHMENTS	SATURDAY 28
WORD COUNT:	MARKETING HOURS:
BRAINSTORMING HOURS:	RESEARCH HOURS:
EDITING HOURS:	READING HOURS:

WEEKLY OVERVIEW

EXERCISE: Take 5-minutes to write something with the 2 words below:

Orange   Rug

Post your exercise on the 4HP Accountable Authors Group on Facebook!

What was your sprint time and top word count?

_____

List a new song you discovered this week:

_____

Favorite food or drink this week:

_____

How did you reward yourself?

_____

What project(s) did you work on?

_____

What are you reading?

_____

What went well this week?

_____

What could improve this week?

_____

_____

_____

TOTAL FOR THE WEEK

Word Count:_____   Marketing Hours:_____
Brainstorming Hours:_____   Research Hours:_____
Editing Hours:_____   Reading Hours:_____

Don't forget to color in your grid!

OCTOBER

The Cheerleader

Writing is sweat and drudgery most of the time. And you have to love it in order to endure the solitude and the discipline.

— Peter Benchley, author of Jaws

THE ARCHITECT

Print out or look at your work in a different font and size during revisions. The new layout will trick your brain into reading your work in a new way, making it easier to catch errors.

THE RESEARCHER

"Good character is not formed in a week or a month. It is created little by little, day by day. Protracted and patient effort is needed to develop good character."

— Heraclitus

THE TASKMASTER

Every mistake is a learning experience. Mistakes teach us to not make the same mistakes, just all new ones.

OCTOBER

213

DAILY ACCOMPLISHMENTS   SUNDAY 29

WORD COUNT:_____   MARKETING HOURS:_____
BRAINSTORMING HOURS:_____   RESEARCH HOURS:_____
EDITING HOURS:_____   READING HOURS:_____

DAILY ACCOMPLISHMENTS   MONDAY 30

WORD COUNT:_____   MARKETING HOURS:_____
BRAINSTORMING HOURS:_____   RESEARCH HOURS:_____
EDITING HOURS:_____   READING HOURS:_____

DAILY ACCOMPLISHMENTS   TUESDAY 31

WORD COUNT:_____   MARKETING HOURS:_____
BRAINSTORMING HOURS:_____   RESEARCH HOURS:_____
EDITING HOURS:_____   READING HOURS:_____

O C T O B E R

THE RESEARCHER

You have two--count them--two months left. It is potentially a time for family, friends, celebrating, and distractions. Do not forgo the festivities; just make sure you still make time for your writing. If you are doing NaNo, may the force be with you.

Weekly Overview

EXERCISE: Take 5-minutes to write something with the 2 words below:

Mythology   Spaghetti

Post your exercise on the 4HP Accountable Authors Group on Facebook!

What was your sprint time and top word count?

_____

List a new song you discovered this week:

_____

Favorite food or drink this week:

_____

How did you reward yourself?

_____

What project(s) did you work on?

_____

What are you reading?

_____

What went well this week?

_____

What could improve this week?

_____

_____

_____

Total for the Week

Word Count:_____   Marketing Hours:_____
Brainstorming Hours:_____   Research Hours:_____
Editing Hours:_____   Reading Hours:_____

Don't forget to color in your grid!

MONTHLY ACTIVITY GRID

OCTOBER

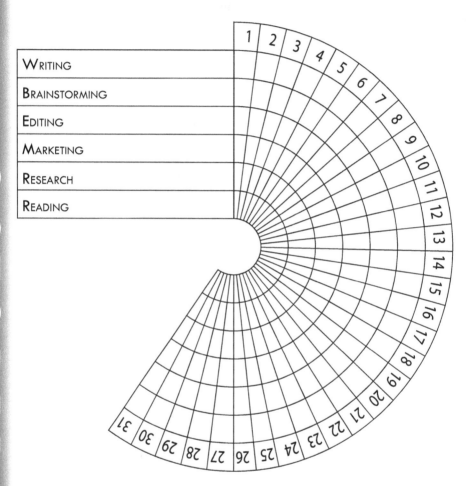

WRITING

BRAINSTORMING

EDITING

MARKETING

RESEARCH

READING

YOUR AVERAGE WORD COUNT FOR THE MONTH

Total Word Count:_____ Divided by _____ days =_____

TOTAL FOR THE YEAR SO FAR

Word Count:_____   Marketing Hours:_____

Brainstorming Hours:_____   Research Hours:_____

Editing Hours:_____   Reading Hours:_____

JOURNAL

What was your **top week**?

_____

What made your **top week** successful?

_____

What was your biggest **obstacle**?

_____

How did you **overcome** this? Or could do better next time?

_____

_____

What was your biggest **achievement**?

_____

_____

What **inspired** you most this month?

_____

Did you **discover** a new writing tip or advice this month?

_____

_____

TOTAL FOR THE MONTH

Word Count:_____   Research Hours:_____
Brainstorming Hours:_____   Reading Hours:_____
Editing Hours:_____
Marketing Hours:_____

TOTAL FOR THE YEAR SO FAR

Word Count:_____   Research Hours:_____
Brainstorming Hours:_____   Reading Hours:_____
Editing Hours:_____
Marketing Hours:_____

Don't forget to color in your grid!

NOVEMBER - NaNoWriMo!

H ere is where you can sign up to participate: nanowrimo.org
"EVERY STORY MATTERS." - NaNoWriMo.org
Let's start writing yours. Writing a novel alone can be difficult, even for seasoned writers. NaNoWriMo helps you track your progress, set milestones, connect with other writers in a vast community, and participate in events that are designed to make sure you finish your novel. Oh, and best of all, it's free!

Native American
Heritage Month
Nov 1 All Saint's Day
Nov 2 All Souls' Day

Nov 3 New York
City Marathon
Nov 5 Election Day

Nov 11 Veterans Day
Nov 28 Thanksgiving
Nov 29 Black Friday

WHAT DOES YOUR MONTH LOOK LIKE

Holidays:_____   Weekends:_____
Weekdays:_____   Other:_____

What **project(s)** do you plan on working on?

_____

What **goal** are you aiming to achieve?

_____

What will be your biggest **obstacle** this month?

_____

How will you **overcome** this? Or adjust for this?

_____

What will be your End of the Month **reward**?

_____

GOALS FOR THIS MONTH

Word Count:_____   Marketing Hours:_____
Brainstorming Hours:_____   Research Hours:_____
Editing Hours:_____   Reading Hours:_____

Week 1

Daily Accomplishments — Wednesday 1

Word Count: _____

Brainstorming Hours: _____

Editing Hours: _____

Marketing Hours: _____

Research Hours: _____

Reading Hours: _____

Daily Accomplishments — Thursday 2

Word Count: _____

Brainstorming Hours: _____

Editing Hours: _____

Marketing Hours: _____

Research Hours: _____

Reading Hours: _____

Daily Accomplishments — Friday 3

Word Count: _____

Brainstorming Hours: _____

Editing Hours: _____

Marketing Hours: _____

Research Hours: _____

Reading Hours: _____

Daily Accomplishments — Saturday 4

Word Count: _____

Brainstorming Hours: _____

Editing Hours: _____

Marketing Hours: _____

Research Hours: _____

Reading Hours: _____

Daily Accomplishments — Sunday 5

Word Count: _____

Brainstorming Hours: _____

Editing Hours: _____

Marketing Hours: _____

Research Hours: _____

Reading Hours: _____

Daily Accomplishments — Monday 6

Word Count: _____

Brainstorming Hours: _____

Editing Hours: _____

Marketing Hours: _____

Research Hours: _____

Reading Hours: _____

Daily Accomplishments — Tuesday 7

Word Count: _____

Brainstorming Hours: _____

Editing Hours: _____

Marketing Hours: _____

Research Hours: _____

Reading Hours: _____

WEEKLY OVERVIEW

EXERCISE: Take 5-minutes to write something with the 2 words below:

Curled   Forge

Post your exercise on the 4HP Accountable Authors Group on Facebook!

What was your sprint time and top word count?

_____

List a new song you discovered this week:

_____

Favorite food or drink this week:

_____

How did you reward yourself?

_____

What project(s) did you work on?

_____

What are you reading?

_____

What went well this week?

_____

What could improve this week?

_____

_____

_____

TOTAL FOR THE WEEK

Word Count:_____   Marketing Hours:_____
Brainstorming Hours:_____   Research Hours:_____
Editing Hours:_____   Reading Hours:_____

Don't forget to color in your grid!

The Cheerleader

"Perfectionism is the voice of the oppressor, the enemy of the people. It will keep you cramped and insane your whole life, and it is the main obstacle between you and a shitty first draft. I think perfectionism is based on the obsessive belief that if you run carefully enough, hitting each stepping-stone just right, you won't have to die. The truth is that you will die anyway and that a lot of people who aren't even looking at their feet are going to do a whole lot better than you, and have a lot more fun while they're doing it."

— Anne Lamott (Bird by Bird: Some
Instructions on Writing and Life)"

THE ARCHITECT

"Long patience and application saturated with your heart's blood—you will either write or you will not—and the only way to find out whether you will or not is to try."

— Jim Tully

THE RESEARCHER

Don't be afraid to use what experience you do have to help create what you don't know. When Stephen Crane was asked how he wrote such realistic battle scenes in the Civil War novel, *The Red Badge of Courage*, despite being born five years after it ended, he claimed playing football taught him everything he needed to know.

THE TASKMASTER

Believe in yourself. Decide you are a great writer--and that's exactly what you will be.

NOVEMBER

223

WEEK 2

DAILY ACCOMPLISHMENTS   **WEDNESDAY 8**

Word Count:_____   Marketing Hours:_____

Brainstorming Hours:_____   Research Hours:_____

Editing Hours:_____   Reading Hours:_____

DAILY ACCOMPLISHMENTS   **THURSDAY 9**

Word Count:_____   Marketing Hours:_____

Brainstorming Hours:_____   Research Hours:_____

Editing Hours:_____   Reading Hours:_____

DAILY ACCOMPLISHMENTS   **FRIDAY 10**

Word Count:_____   Marketing Hours:_____

Brainstorming Hours:_____   Research Hours:_____

Editing Hours:_____   Reading Hours:_____

DAILY ACCOMPLISHMENTS   **SATURDAY 11**

Word Count:_____   Marketing Hours:_____

Brainstorming Hours:_____   Research Hours:_____

Editing Hours:_____   Reading Hours:_____

DAILY ACCOMPLISHMENTS   **SUNDAY 12**

Word Count:_____   Marketing Hours:_____

Brainstorming Hours:_____   Research Hours:_____

Editing Hours:_____   Reading Hours:_____

DAILY ACCOMPLISHMENTS   **MONDAY 13**

Word Count:_____   Marketing Hours:_____

Brainstorming Hours:_____   Research Hours:_____

Editing Hours:_____   Reading Hours:_____

DAILY ACCOMPLISHMENTS   **TUESDAY 14**

Word Count:_____   Marketing Hours:_____

Brainstorming Hours:_____   Research Hours:_____

Editing Hours:_____   Reading Hours:_____

WEEKLY OVERVIEW

EXERCISE: Take 5-minutes to write something with the 2 words below:

Journey   Towel

Post your exercise on the 4HP Accountable Authors Group on Facebook!

What was your sprint time and top word count?

_____

List a new song you discovered this week:

_____

Favorite food or drink this week:

_____

How did you reward yourself?

_____

What project(s) did you work on?

_____

What are you reading?

_____

What went well this week?

_____

What could improve this week?

_____

_____

_____

TOTAL FOR THE WEEK

Word Count:_____   Marketing Hours:_____
Brainstorming Hours:_____   Research Hours:_____
Editing Hours:_____   Reading Hours:_____

Don't forget to color in your grid!

NOVEMBER

The Cheerleader

Follow two other writers on social media who are participating in Nanowrimo. If they can do it, so can you!

THE ARCHITECT

What's the best fictional death you've read in a story? What made this so epic? What was the worst death? Why? What lessons from these impressions can you apply to your writing?

226

THE RESEARCHER

Where do we hide the body? How do we get rid of it? Was this murder, or just a corpse found that complicates life? Poor William Hazlitt, a 19th century critic, had his body stuffed underneath his bed so his London landlady could start showing the room to potential renters. WOW.

THE TASKMASTER

Stop wasting time on social media or watching Netflix. Get back to the part where you are creating worlds.

Week 3

DAILY ACCOMPLISHMENTS	**WEDNESDAY 15**
Word Count:	*Marketing Hours:*
Brainstorming Hours:	*Research Hours:*
Editing Hours:	*Reading Hours:*

DAILY ACCOMPLISHMENTS	**THURSDAY 16**
Word Count:	*Marketing Hours:*
Brainstorming Hours:	*Research Hours:*
Editing Hours:	*Reading Hours:*

DAILY ACCOMPLISHMENTS	**FRIDAY 17**
Word Count:	*Marketing Hours:*
Brainstorming Hours:	*Research Hours:*
Editing Hours:	*Reading Hours:*

DAILY ACCOMPLISHMENTS	**SATURDAY 18**
Word Count:	*Marketing Hours:*
Brainstorming Hours:	*Research Hours:*
Editing Hours:	*Reading Hours:*

DAILY ACCOMPLISHMENTS	**SUNDAY 19**
Word Count:	*Marketing Hours:*
Brainstorming Hours:	*Research Hours:*
Editing Hours:	*Reading Hours:*

DAILY ACCOMPLISHMENTS	**MONDAY 20**
Word Count:	*Marketing Hours:*
Brainstorming Hours:	*Research Hours:*
Editing Hours:	*Reading Hours:*

DAILY ACCOMPLISHMENTS	**TUESDAY 21**
Word Count:	*Marketing Hours:*
Brainstorming Hours:	*Research Hours:*
Editing Hours:	*Reading Hours:*

WEEKLY OVERVIEW

EXERCISE: Take 5-minutes to write something with the 2 words below:

Smooth   Publish

Post your exercise on the 4HP Accountable Authors Group on Facebook!

What was your sprint time and top word count?

_____

List a new song you discovered this week:

_____

Favorite food or drink this week:

_____

How did you reward yourself?

_____

What project(s) did you work on?

_____

What are you reading?

_____

What went well this week?

_____

What could improve this week?

_____

_____

_____

TOTAL FOR THE WEEK

Word Count:_____   Marketing Hours:_____
Brainstorming Hours:_____   Research Hours:_____
Editing Hours:_____   Reading Hours:_____

Don't forget to color in your grid!

NOVEMBER

The Cheerleader

Post the cover of your current project on the 4HP Accountable Authors group on Facebook. Don't have one? Share one of your favorite covers and tell us why!

THE ARCHITECT

Don't edit as you write. It will only slow down the drafting process. You can make it pretty later. Focus on getting the words out right now.

THE RESEARCHER

"To know what people really think, pay regard to what they do rather than what they say."

— René Descartes

THE TASKMASTER

Ctrl Find "shrug," "nod," "sigh," and any other words you use too frequently and clean that crap up!

WEEK 4

DAILY ACCOMPLISHMENTS	**WEDNESDAY 22**
Word Count:	Marketing Hours:
Brainstorming Hours:	Research Hours:
Editing Hours:	Reading Hours:

DAILY ACCOMPLISHMENTS	**THURSDAY 23**
Word Count:	Marketing Hours:
Brainstorming Hours:	Research Hours:
Editing Hours:	Reading Hours:

DAILY ACCOMPLISHMENTS	**FRIDAY 24**
Word Count:	Marketing Hours:
Brainstorming Hours:	Research Hours:
Editing Hours:	Reading Hours:

DAILY ACCOMPLISHMENTS	**SATURDAY 25**
Word Count:	Marketing Hours:
Brainstorming Hours:	Research Hours:
Editing Hours:	Reading Hours:

DAILY ACCOMPLISHMENTS	**SUNDAY 26**
Word Count:	Marketing Hours:
Brainstorming Hours:	Research Hours:
Editing Hours:	Reading Hours:

DAILY ACCOMPLISHMENTS	**MONDAY 27**
Word Count:	Marketing Hours:
Brainstorming Hours:	Research Hours:
Editing Hours:	Reading Hours:

DAILY ACCOMPLISHMENTS	**TUESDAY 28**
Word Count:	Marketing Hours:
Brainstorming Hours:	Research Hours:
Editing Hours:	Reading Hours:

Weekly Overview

EXERCISE: Take 5-minutes to write something with the 2 words below:

Limousine   Athlete

Post your exercise on the 4HP Accountable Authors Group on Facebook!

What was your sprint time and top word count?

_____

List a new song you discovered this week:

_____

Favorite food or drink this week:

_____

How did you reward yourself?

_____

What project(s) did you work on?

_____

What are you reading?

_____

What went well this week?

_____

What could improve this week?

_____

_____

_____

TOTAL FOR THE WEEK

Word Count:_____   Marketing Hours:_____
Brainstorming Hours:_____   Research Hours:_____
Editing Hours:_____   Reading Hours:_____

Don't forget to color in your grid!

NOVEMBER

The Cheerleader

A spoonful of sugar helps the medicine go down. Record one sweet thing that offsets one negative thing this week.

THE ARCHITECT

"Plot is people. Human emotions and desires founded on the realities of life, working at cross purposes, getting hotter and fiercer as they strike against each other until finally there's an explosion—that's Plot."

— *Leigh Brackett*

234

THE RESEARCHER

Think of all the options and imagine how they change the tone of your story. Letters from Edgar Allen Poe reveal how he considered using an owl or even a parrot to say "*nevermore*" until he found the raven.

THE TASKMASTER

You are expected to fail. We will all fail many times in our lives. It's what you do with that failure that makes the difference. Learn from it.

DAILY ACCOMPLISHMENTS

WEDNESDAY 29

WORD COUNT:_____

MARKETING HOURS:_____

BRAINSTORMING HOURS:_____

RESEARCH HOURS:_____

EDITING HOURS:_____

READING HOURS:_____

DAILY ACCOMPLISHMENTS

THURSDAY 30

WORD COUNT:_____

MARKETING HOURS:_____

BRAINSTORMING HOURS:_____

RESEARCH HOURS:_____

EDITING HOURS:_____

READING HOURS:_____

The Cheerleader

Your world doesn't have to make sense! Trust me, the one we live in can be unpredictable and full of strange settings. In Centralia, Pennsylvania, you can find a true American "ghost" town. The strange part? It's has an underground fire that is still burning! It started in 1962 when the town set fire to the local dump to "clean it up" only to set fire to the coal mine beneath the town. You can still see smoke rising through the cracks on the roads!

Weekly Overview

EXERCISE: Take 5-minutes to write something with the 2 words below:

Headset   Tail

Post your exercise on the 4HP Accountable Authors Group on Facebook!

What was your sprint time and top word count?

_____

List a new song you discovered this week:

_____

Favorite food or drink this week:

_____

How did you reward yourself?

_____

What project(s) did you work on?

_____

What are you reading?

_____

What went well this week?

_____

What could improve this week?

_____

_____

_____

Total for the Week

Word Count:_____   Marketing Hours:_____
Brainstorming Hours:_____   Research Hours:_____
Editing Hours:_____   Reading Hours:_____

Don't forget to color in your grid!

MONTHLY ACTIVITY GRID

NOVEMBER

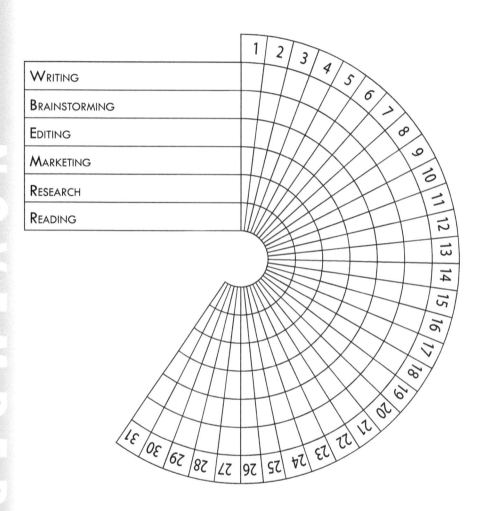

WRITING

BRAINSTORMING

EDITING

MARKETING

RESEARCH

READING

YOUR AVERAGE WORD COUNT FOR THE MONTH

Total Word Count:_____ Divided by _____ days =_____

TOTAL FOR THE YEAR SO FAR

Word Count:_____ Marketing Hours:_____

Brainstorming Hours:_____ Research Hours:_____

Editing Hours:_____ Reading Hours:_____

JOURNAL

What was your **top week**?

_____

What made your **top week** successful?

_____

What was your biggest **obstacle**?

_____

How did you **overcome** this? Or could do better next time?

_____

_____

What was your biggest **achievement**?

_____

_____

What **inspired** you most this month?

_____

Did you **discover** a new writing tip or advice this month?

_____

_____

TOTAL FOR THE MONTH

Word Count:_____   Marketing Hours:_____
Brainstorming Hours:_____   Research Hours:_____
Editing Hours:_____   Reading Hours:_____

TOTAL FOR THE YEAR SO FAR

Word Count:_____   Marketing Hours:_____
Brainstorming Hours:_____   Research Hours:_____
Editing Hours:_____   Reading Hours:_____

240   *Don't forget to color in your grid!*

DECEMBER

Okay. Breathe. You survived NANO (if you participated). We are in the home stretch. You need to double your efforts (or enjoy the feeling of attaining goals early), review your goal for the month (and year), and make sure you cross that finish line. This month is filled with distractions like food-filled holidays. Make sure you plan your productive and enjoyment time equally. Keep the momentum going right into next year!

Dec 6 St. Nicholas Day
Dec 7 Pearl Harbor
Remembrance Day

Dec 15 The
Architect's Birthday
Dec 21 December Solstice

Dec 24 Christmas Eve
Dec 25 Christmas Day
Dec 31 New Year's Eve

WHAT DOES YOUR MONTH LOOK LIKE

Holidays:_____   Weekends:_____

Weekdays:_____   Other:_____

What **project(s)** do you plan on working on?

_____

What **goal** are you aiming to achieve?

_____

What will be your biggest **obstacle** this month?

_____

How will you **overcome** this? Or adjust for this?

_____

What will be your End of the Month **reward**?

_____

GOALS FOR THIS MONTH

Word Count:_____   Marketing Hours:_____

Brainstorming Hours:_____   Research Hours:_____

Editing Hours:_____   Reading Hours:_____

Week 1

DAILY ACCOMPLISHMENTS   **FRIDAY 1**

WORD COUNT:_____   MARKETING HOURS:_____
BRAINSTORMING HOURS:_____   RESEARCH HOURS:_____
EDITING HOURS:_____   READING HOURS:_____

DAILY ACCOMPLISHMENTS   **SATURDAY 2**

WORD COUNT:_____   MARKETING HOURS:_____
BRAINSTORMING HOURS:_____   RESEARCH HOURS:_____
EDITING HOURS:_____   READING HOURS:_____

DAILY ACCOMPLISHMENTS   **SUNDAY 3**

WORD COUNT:_____   MARKETING HOURS:_____
BRAINSTORMING HOURS:_____   RESEARCH HOURS:_____
EDITING HOURS:_____   READING HOURS:_____

DAILY ACCOMPLISHMENTS   **MONDAY 4**

WORD COUNT:_____   MARKETING HOURS:_____
BRAINSTORMING HOURS:_____   RESEARCH HOURS:_____
EDITING HOURS:_____   READING HOURS:_____

DAILY ACCOMPLISHMENTS   **TUESDAY 5**

WORD COUNT:_____   MARKETING HOURS:_____
BRAINSTORMING HOURS:_____   RESEARCH HOURS:_____
EDITING HOURS:_____   READING HOURS:_____

DAILY ACCOMPLISHMENTS   **WEDNESDAY 6**

WORD COUNT:_____   MARKETING HOURS:_____
BRAINSTORMING HOURS:_____   RESEARCH HOURS:_____
EDITING HOURS:_____   READING HOURS:_____

DAILY ACCOMPLISHMENTS   **THURSDAY 7**

WORD COUNT:_____   MARKETING HOURS:_____
BRAINSTORMING HOURS:_____   RESEARCH HOURS:_____
EDITING HOURS:_____   READING HOURS:_____

Weekly Overview

EXERCISE: Take 5-minutes to write something with the 2 words below:

Elephant   Notebook

Post your exercise on the 4HP Accountable Authors Group on Facebook!

What was your sprint time and top word count?

_____

List a new song you discovered this week:

_____

Favorite food or drink this week:

_____

How did you reward yourself?

_____

What project(s) did you work on?

_____

What are you reading?

_____

What went well this week?

_____

What could improve this week?

_____

_____

_____

Total for the Week

Word Count:_____   Marketing Hours:_____
Brainstorming Hours:_____   Research Hours:_____
Editing Hours:_____   Reading Hours:_____

Don't forget to color in your grid!

The Cheerleader

"You may not always write well, but you can edit a bad page. You can't edit a blank page."

— Jodi Picoult

THE ARCHITECT

"One thing that helps is to give myself permission to write badly. I tell myself that I'm going to do my five or ten pages no matter what, and that I can always tear them up the following morning if I want. I'll have lost nothing—writing and tearing up five pages would leave me no further behind than if I took the day off."

— Lawrence Block

DECEMBER

The Researcher

My dog ate my homework. No, really--this happens to people among other humorous scenarios, so use them in your storytelling in unique ways. I mean, John Steinbeck's first draft of *Of Mice and Men* was torn to shreds by his dog. He later joked to a friend it was a sign it needed revisions.

THE TASKMASTER

MORE WORDS!!! I'm sure if I asked, you could add a few more words on that page. I'm asking-- actually, I am TELLING you. Go back in there.

DECEMBER

DAILY ACCOMPLISHMENTS   **FRIDAY 8**

WORD COUNT:_____   MARKETING HOURS:_____
BRAINSTORMING HOURS:_____   RESEARCH HOURS:_____
EDITING HOURS:_____   READING HOURS:_____

DAILY ACCOMPLISHMENTS   **SATURDAY 9**

WORD COUNT:_____   MARKETING HOURS:_____
BRAINSTORMING HOURS:_____   RESEARCH HOURS:_____
EDITING HOURS:_____   READING HOURS:_____

DAILY ACCOMPLISHMENTS   **SUNDAY 10**

WORD COUNT:_____   MARKETING HOURS:_____
BRAINSTORMING HOURS:_____   RESEARCH HOURS:_____
EDITING HOURS:_____   READING HOURS:_____

DAILY ACCOMPLISHMENTS   **MONDAY 11**

WORD COUNT:_____   MARKETING HOURS:_____
BRAINSTORMING HOURS:_____   RESEARCH HOURS:_____
EDITING HOURS:_____   READING HOURS:_____

DAILY ACCOMPLISHMENTS   **TUESDAY 12**

WORD COUNT:_____   MARKETING HOURS:_____
BRAINSTORMING HOURS:_____   RESEARCH HOURS:_____
EDITING HOURS:_____   READING HOURS:_____

DAILY ACCOMPLISHMENTS   **WEDNESDAY 13**

WORD COUNT:_____   MARKETING HOURS:_____
BRAINSTORMING HOURS:_____   RESEARCH HOURS:_____
EDITING HOURS:_____   READING HOURS:_____

DAILY ACCOMPLISHMENTS   **THURSDAY 14**

WORD COUNT:_____   MARKETING HOURS:_____
BRAINSTORMING HOURS:_____   RESEARCH HOURS:_____
EDITING HOURS:_____   READING HOURS:_____

DECEMBER

Weekly Overview

EXERCISE: Take 5-minutes to write something with the 2 words below:

Photograph   Soundtrack

Post your exercise on the 4HP Accountable Authors Group on Facebook!

What was your sprint time and top word count?

_____

List a new song you discovered this week:

_____

Favorite food or drink this week:

_____

How did you reward yourself?

_____

What project(s) did you work on?

_____

What are you reading?

_____

What went well this week?

_____

What could improve this week?

_____

_____

_____

Total for the Week

Word Count:_____   Marketing Hours:_____
Brainstorming Hours:_____   Research Hours:_____
Editing Hours:_____   Reading Hours:_____

Don't forget to color in your grid!

DECEMBER

The Cheerleader

Treat yourself this week! Meet up with writers at a cafe or online for an hour long writing session.

THE ARCHITECT

Are you telling the right character's story? Try flipping it out and write a scene from a different character's point-of-view! For example, telling a story from the POV of a shark, the diver, or even the boat can differ drastically!

THE RESEARCHER

"Although you may spend your life killing, you will not exhaust all your foes. But if you quell your own anger, your real enemy will be slain."

— Nagarjuna

THE TASKMASTER

Have you been practicing your book's elevator pitch? Do it some more, and polish it, even if it is not finished yet. You need to be able to say it in your sleep.

DECEMBER

DAILY ACCOMPLISHMENTS   **FRIDAY 15**

WORD COUNT:_____
MARKETING HOURS:_____
BRAINSTORMING HOURS:_____
RESEARCH HOURS:_____
EDITING HOURS:_____
READING HOURS:_____

DAILY ACCOMPLISHMENTS   **SATURDAY 16**

WORD COUNT:_____
MARKETING HOURS:_____
BRAINSTORMING HOURS:_____
RESEARCH HOURS:_____
EDITING HOURS:_____
READING HOURS:_____

DAILY ACCOMPLISHMENTS   **SUNDAY 17**

WORD COUNT:_____
MARKETING HOURS:_____
BRAINSTORMING HOURS:_____
RESEARCH HOURS:_____
EDITING HOURS:_____
READING HOURS:_____

DAILY ACCOMPLISHMENTS   **MONDAY 18**

WORD COUNT:_____
MARKETING HOURS:_____
BRAINSTORMING HOURS:_____
RESEARCH HOURS:_____
EDITING HOURS:_____
READING HOURS:_____

DAILY ACCOMPLISHMENTS   **TUESDAY 19**

WORD COUNT:_____
MARKETING HOURS:_____
BRAINSTORMING HOURS:_____
RESEARCH HOURS:_____
EDITING HOURS:_____
READING HOURS:_____

DAILY ACCOMPLISHMENTS   **WEDNESDAY 20**

WORD COUNT:_____
MARKETING HOURS:_____
BRAINSTORMING HOURS:_____
RESEARCH HOURS:_____
EDITING HOURS:_____
READING HOURS:_____

DAILY ACCOMPLISHMENTS   **THURSDAY 21**

WORD COUNT:_____
MARKETING HOURS:_____
BRAINSTORMING HOURS:_____
RESEARCH HOURS:_____
EDITING HOURS:_____
READING HOURS:_____

DECEMBER

Weekly Overview

EXERCISE: Take 5-minutes to write something with the 2 words below:

Spooky   Gelatin

Post your exercise on the 4HP Accountable Authors Group on Facebook!

What was your sprint time and top word count?

_____

List a new song you discovered this week:

_____

Favorite food or drink this week:

_____

How did you reward yourself?

_____

What project(s) did you work on?

_____

What are you reading?

_____

What went well this week?

_____

What could improve this week?

_____

_____

_____

Total for the Week

Word Count:_____   Marketing Hours:_____
Brainstorming Hours:_____   Research Hours:_____
Editing Hours:_____   Reading Hours:_____

Don't forget to color in your grid!

The Cheerleader

The Doctor Is In: What struggles are your characters facing right now? Work through the issues here.

THE ARCHITECT

"Write. Rewrite. When not writing or rewriting, read. I know of no shortcuts."

— *Larry L. King*

THE RESEARCHER

Art begets art. Writers, musicians, and artists inspire one another often. Do you have a pin board or playlist? William Golding's masterpiece *Lord of the Flies* has inspired music from famous bands like U2 and Iron Maiden.

THE TASKMASTER

Editors are your friends. They are not your nice friends. They can be downright mean sometimes. They are simply making your work better. Remember that.

DECEMBER

DAILY ACCOMPLISHMENTS   **FRIDAY 22**

WORD COUNT:_____   MARKETING HOURS:_____
BRAINSTORMING HOURS:_____   RESEARCH HOURS:_____
EDITING HOURS:_____   READING HOURS:_____

DAILY ACCOMPLISHMENTS   **SATURDAY 23**

WORD COUNT:_____   MARKETING HOURS:_____
BRAINSTORMING HOURS:_____   RESEARCH HOURS:_____
EDITING HOURS:_____   READING HOURS:_____

DAILY ACCOMPLISHMENTS   **SUNDAY 24**

WORD COUNT:_____   MARKETING HOURS:_____
BRAINSTORMING HOURS:_____   RESEARCH HOURS:_____
EDITING HOURS:_____   READING HOURS:_____

DAILY ACCOMPLISHMENTS   **MONDAY 25**

WORD COUNT:_____   MARKETING HOURS:_____
BRAINSTORMING HOURS:_____   RESEARCH HOURS:_____
EDITING HOURS:_____   READING HOURS:_____

DAILY ACCOMPLISHMENTS   **TUESDAY 26**

WORD COUNT:_____   MARKETING HOURS:_____
BRAINSTORMING HOURS:_____   RESEARCH HOURS:_____
EDITING HOURS:_____   READING HOURS:_____

DAILY ACCOMPLISHMENTS   **WEDNESDAY 27**

WORD COUNT:_____   MARKETING HOURS:_____
BRAINSTORMING HOURS:_____   RESEARCH HOURS:_____
EDITING HOURS:_____   READING HOURS:_____

DAILY ACCOMPLISHMENTS   **THURSDAY 28**

WORD COUNT:_____   MARKETING HOURS:_____
BRAINSTORMING HOURS:_____   RESEARCH HOURS:_____
EDITING HOURS:_____   READING HOURS:_____

WEEKLY OVERVIEW

EXERCISE: Take 5-minutes to write something with the 2 words below:

Snowman   Scissors

Post your exercise on the 4HP Accountable Authors Group on Facebook!

What was your sprint time and top word count?

_____

List a new song you discovered this week:

_____

Favorite food or drink this week:

_____

How did you reward yourself?

_____

What project(s) did you work on?

_____

What are you reading?

_____

What went well this week?

_____

What could improve this week?

_____

_____

_____

TOTAL FOR THE WEEK

Word Count:_____   Marketing Hours:_____
Brainstorming Hours:_____   Research Hours:_____
Editing Hours:_____   Reading Hours:_____

Don't forget to color in your grid!

DECEMBER

255

The Cheerleader

"*To gain your own voice, you have to forget about having it heard.*"
— Allen Ginsberg

"

THE ARCHITECT

Review your writing from this year. What was your favorite story, moment, scene, or snippet of dialogue?

DECEMBER

THE RESEARCHER

What have you been watching? Many authors treat themselves to watching movies or binging shows and that's okay! Kurt Vonnegut, author of *Slaughterhouse-Five*, was a huge fan of Cheers. He later claimed he would gladly give up his novels to have tried his hand at scriptwriting for television shows.

THE TASKMASTER

Hero to Zero. Start each day with a goal. When you achieve it, celebrate for a moment, then start again.

DECEMBER

257

DAILY ACCOMPLISHMENTS   **THURSDAY 29**

WORD COUNT:_____   MARKETING HOURS:_____
BRAINSTORMING HOURS:_____   RESEARCH HOURS:_____
EDITING HOURS:_____   READING HOURS:_____

DAILY ACCOMPLISHMENTS   **FRIDAY 30**

WORD COUNT:_____   MARKETING HOURS:_____
BRAINSTORMING HOURS:_____   RESEARCH HOURS:_____
EDITING HOURS:_____   READING HOURS:_____

DAILY ACCOMPLISHMENTS   **SATURDAY 31**

WORD COUNT:_____   MARKETING HOURS:_____
BRAINSTORMING HOURS:_____   RESEARCH HOURS:_____
EDITING HOURS:_____   READING HOURS:_____

THE ARCHITECT
How would you describe your writing style?
Pantser, Plotter, Plantser, or Chaostitian?

I hope you consider yourself a badass! I know
I do. YOU DID IT! You made it to the end
of this book. Now grab next year's version and
start again.

D E C E M B E R

WEEKLY OVERVIEW

EXERCISE: Take 5-minutes to write something with the 2 words below:

Goose   Bottle

Post your exercise on the 4HP Accountable Authors Group on Facebook!

What was your sprint time and top word count?

_____

List a new song you discovered this week:

_____

Favorite food or drink this week:

_____

How did you reward yourself?

_____

What project(s) did you work on?

_____

What are you reading?

_____

What went well this week?

_____

What could improve this week?

_____

_____

_____

TOTAL FOR THE WEEK

Word Count:_____ Marketing Hours:_____
Brainstorming Hours:_____ Research Hours:_____
Editing Hours:_____ Reading Hours:_____

Don't forget to color in your grid!

MONTHLY ACTIVITY GRID

DECEMBER

WRITING OR WORD COUNT

BRAINSTORMING

EDITING

MARKETING OR SOCIAL MEDIA

RESEARCH

READING

OTHER:

1 2 3 4 5 6 7 8 9 10 11 12 13 14 15 16 17 18 19 20 21 22 23 24 25 26 27 28 29 30 31

YOUR AVERAGE WORD COUNT FOR THE MONTH

Total Word Count:_____ Divided by _____ days =_____

TOTAL FOR THE YEAR

Word Count:_____   Marketing Hours:_____
Brainstorming Hours:_____   Research Hours:_____
Editing Hours:_____   Reading Hours:_____

JOURNAL

What was your **top week**?

_____

What made your **top week** successful?

_____

What was your biggest **obstacle**?

_____

How did you **overcome** this? Or could do better next time?

_____

_____

What was your biggest **achievement**?

_____

_____

What **inspired** you most this month?

_____

Did you **discover** a new writing tip or advice this month?

_____

_____

TOTAL FOR THE MONTH

Word Count:_____   Marketing Hours:_____
Brainstorming Hours:_____   Research Hours:_____
Editing Hours:_____   Reading Hours:_____

TOTAL FOR THE YEAR SO FAR

Word Count:_____   Marketing Hours:_____
Brainstorming Hours:_____   Research Hours:_____
Editing Hours:_____   Reading Hours:_____

Don't forget to color in your grid!

The year is
Officially OVER!

Great job
staying accountable!

Time for your
Yearly Review!

YEARLY GRID BY ACTIVITY

N ow, let's see what your activity looks like! This grid is designed to reveal what activities you do most in regards to the month or season even. You may be surprised that you do more writing at the start or end of the year. Take a moment and really pay attention to what you did, when you did it, and how you can best set your goals for the next year!

☐	WRITING
☐	BRAINSTORMING
☐	EDITING
☐	MARKETING
☐	RESEARCH
☐	READING
☐	OTHER:
☐	OTHER:
☐	OTHER:

YOUR AVERAGE WORD COUNT FOR THE YEAR

Total Word Count:_____ Divided by 365 =_____

What area did you spend the most time on?

_____

_____

What area should you work on n?

_____

_____

	J	F	M	A	M	J	J	A	S	O	N	D
1												
2												
3												
4												
5												
6												
7												
8												
9												
10												
11												
12												
13												
14												
15												
16												
17												
18												
19												
20												
21												
22												
23												
24												
25												
26												
27												
28												
29		■										
30												
31		■		■		■			■		■	

YEARLY GRID BY PROJECT

Let's take a look at your projects. If you were wondering why we were asking about this, we want to not only wanted to hold you accountable, but reveal some insight on how long it takes to complete them and how much of your year was spent on each one. Self-evaluation is important for prepping your goals for the year to come and also reveals about how much you really can do in the time you have. You might surprise yourself with the end result here!

☐ _____

☐ _____

☐ _____

☐ _____

☐ _____

☐ _____

☐ _____

☐ _____

☐ _____

☐ _____

What project did you spend the most time on?

_____

_____

Was this a bigger project or more difficult to complete?

_____

_____

	J	F	M	A	M	J	J	A	S	O	N	D
1												
2												
3												
4												
5												
6												
7												
8												
9												
10												
11												
12												
13												
14												
15												
16												
17												
18												
19												
20												
21												
22												
23												
24												
25												
26												
27												
28												
29		■										
30		■										
31		■		■		■			■		■	

THE YEAR IN REVIEW

THE RECKONING

How did you do? Did you do better or worse than expected?

_____

What prize or punishment did you award yourself?

_____

CAPTURE THE NOW

How do you feel right now?

_____

What are you wearing right now, Jake from State Farm? Where are you? Record this moment for Future You to enjoy.

_____

REFLECTION TIME

What habits or practices worked for you this year? Why do you think those worked for you?

_____

What obstacles did you struggle to overcome? How can you address those in the future?

_____

What lessons did you learn this year?

_____

FINAL THOUGHTS

Advice for your Former Self: What would you say now to Old You?

_____

Advice for your Future Self: What would you say to Future You?

_____

TOP TEN

"And remember, this is for posterity, so... be honest."
                              --Count Rugen (The Princess Bride)

1. Best song:_____

2. Best TV show:_____

3. Best movie:_____

4. Best book:_____

5. Best writing moment:_____

6. Best dialogue line:_____

7. Best tips/advice:_____

8. Best life moment:_____

9. Best writing spot:_____

10. Best drink/food:_____

So I Failed... Now What?

You keep writing, that's what you do. Get back on the path and keep going. But it's probably a good time to reevaluate your goals. What is a more reasonable goal for you? Think about the reasons that caused you to fail this time. What can you do differently next time? What are some unanticipated issues you ran into this time? Why didn't you think they would be obstacles? What can you do to prevent more obstacles from knocking you off the writing path?

So I'm finished... Now What?

Yay!!! Cheer one more time for the level of amazingness that is you! Enjoy that sweet reward. You earned this. Relish the moment. Remember this feeling. (Maybe even write down how you feel right now, so you can remind Future You of what is possible.) Now, set the bar a little higher and push yourself to grow or attempt to hit the same goals twice in a row!

Keep that magic going. Keep doing what worked for you this time, and use it to write the next project. Create new rewards and punishments. Plan a new project. Get lost in another world that demands to be poured onto the page. Take note of what worked and what didn't. Like, literally write it down. Use those notes as a record of your writing journey. People change, and so does writing. Allow yourself to see the path you've been on (while looking forward to what comes next).

NEXT YEAR PREP

What projects do you want to complete next year?

_____

_____

_____

_____

_____

Make your Reading List for next year.

_____

_____

_____

_____

_____

Stay accountable

and grab the next edition!

You can always find the best place to grab a copy at

www.4horsemenpublications.com